The Futures & Options Strategy Cheat Code

Mantric Strategies that will
always always protect you

Strategies to be smart so that the
Operators cannot get you

JK BULL

First Published in **August 2024**

ISBN: 978-93-6356-944-7

PUBLISHING MONGERS

+91 9311101365

Distributed by: Watergies

Preface

The Futures and Options strategies that will always be standing by your side and will bring around even time to play on your side without letting you fall in any traps.

Foreword

This book is a way to navigate everyone that is out to get you. If you stick to what the author tells you, you will always be protected. You will navigate all the traps and understand what it means to play the market.

Acknowledgments

A heartfelt thanks to the publishing team for everything you have done for The Futures and Options Strategy Cheat Code.

About the author

I could be someone who is speaking from experience, or I am someone who has learnt from the best, but I might be someone who is involved with the operators, and is somewhat tired of how they play you. I cannot say any more than that. Understanding the game is upto you. Take it or leave it.

Dedication

This one is yet again dedicated to everyone who has lost even a single cent in the market.

Introduction

You are playing against yourself, and no one else in the market, but many factors decide whether you win or you lose. One of the most important ones being time, use it to not let you lose in the market by making it play on your side. Stick to these strategies to achieve your desired goal and you will never lose again. Your positions will always be hedged, protecting you against the worst possible scenarios and your gain a surety. Think of a market where you can gain everything, but in the worst case scenario not lose it all. Give it a try, and you will never look elsewhere. It is time you know The Futures and Options Strategy Cheat Code

Prologue

But, what if there was a way to replicate your futures with options and that too with a loss cap if you are wrong ..

When you think the market is going to go up, you usually buy a Call option. The market might be heading there, but it might just not be ready yet, it might take a few days and with theta decay, you don't earn anything.

How about you trade where you earn whenever the market heads in your direction without losing money when it takes time. How about you get time to play on your side ?

No, option selling is not the way to get there because it is the easiest way to wipe off your capital. Option buying will give you gains, but it will take it all away, that too in one go.

Learn these strategies and you will never lose money again when the market follows your direction no matter how long it takes, and in some cases you will earn even if the market does not follow your direction.

Bullish

If you are bullish on the market, and the market is heading your way but there is a profit booking or maybe it encounters a resistance. Maybe even a bad result in the market or GDP data causes an obstacle, you are bound to lose money. But, not if you follow these strategies and hedge your positions. You will know the maximum you can lose and you can exit whenever you want when you are in green. The more time the market takes to get there, the more you will earn.

Bullish Strategy

Call Spread

Let's say you are expecting the market to go up from this point, but the bears are at work and they are not letting the market go up just yet. It will head there, maybe even with a breakout but it is encountering some resistance. You cannot buy a call option, the decay is going to keep eating at you until the market moves there. But, with this strategy no matter when the market heads in your direction, you will earn. Not only that, the longer it takes, the more you earn.

What do you do ?

You buy a call option at the current spot price and sell a call option four slots above the spot price. The choice is yours. This gives you optimum risk coverage and good profits. You can increase the sell more, and it will fetch you better profits, but you have to be sure how far are you expecting the market to move. You will start earning as soon as the market moves even a point upwards in most cases, but the choice is yours about how far you want to go and how long do you want to wait because you will be earning more every second, every minute and every day.

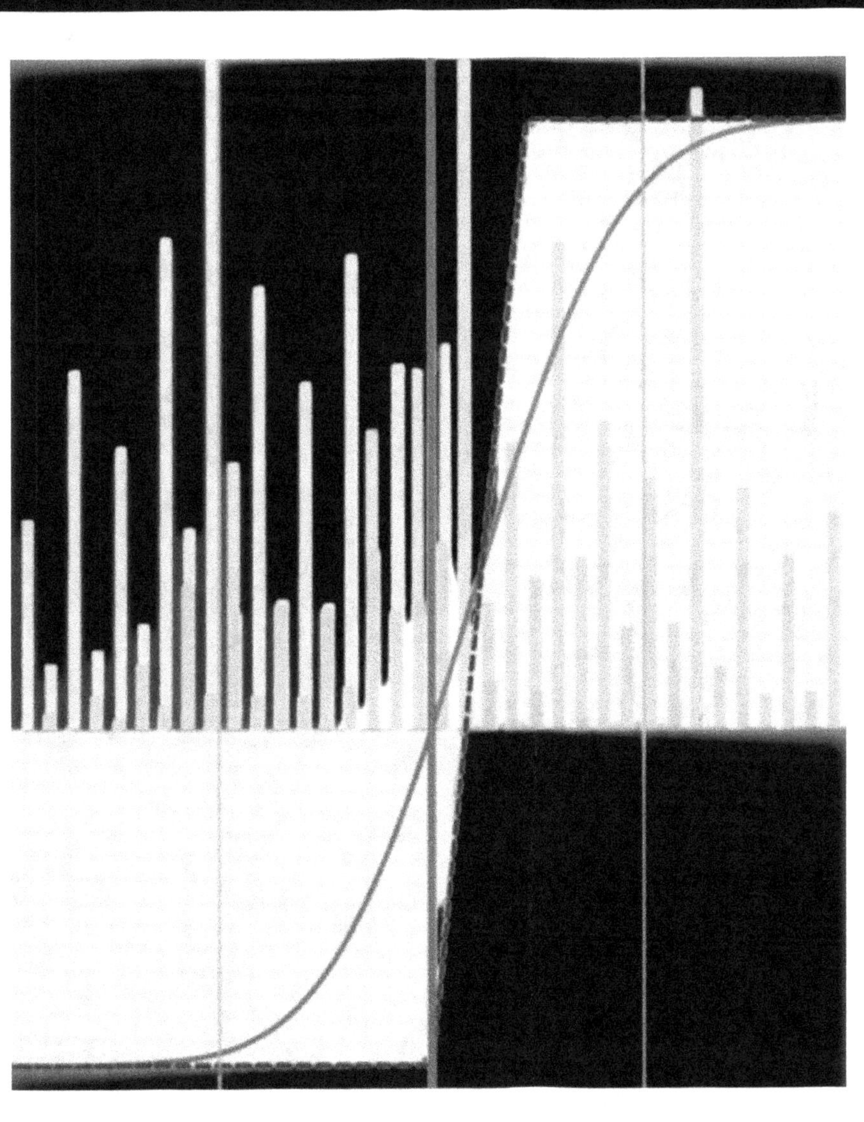

In the graph, you can see that as soon as the market starts heading in your direction, you start earning. The diagonal across line denotes the profit and loss for the day you are making your trade on while the dotted line denotes the profit and loss on expiry. The centre line is the spot price at which the market currently is. In this strategy, you know your maximum loss which is capped no matter what happens in the world. And, if you are right about the direction of the market, the market will reward you, no matter how long it takes before expiry.

Bullish Strategy

Put Spread

Call spread helped you play with the call options to not let theta decay incur any losses to you. Now the put spread helps you to do the same. The loss, if you are wrong is more in comparison to profit, but it helps you earn even if you are just a little wrong. It protects you for some points on the downside even if your trade is bullish. So, if you are expecting flat to positive bias, this might be a better strategy for you. We will go through various strategies with its pros and cons, but the choice in the market will be yours. You will have to decide what is the likely scenario, what is the outcome you are expecting, how much you want to risk, how much you want to earn, when do you want to enter, when do you want to exit and most of all, what works for you.

What do you do ?

You sell a put option at the current market price and buy a put option four slots below. Again, buying the put below is your choice depending on how much downside you want to cover and how much are you willing to risk. The lower you go with buying your put option, the more downside protection you will get while increasing the loss if the market breaches that range. You need to have a range in mind before you get into the range. Deciding on the expiry is also your call. Whether you want to do it in this week's expiry, next week's expiry, monthly expiry or even another month down the road. None of these are wrong, but you need to play with what you are comfortable.

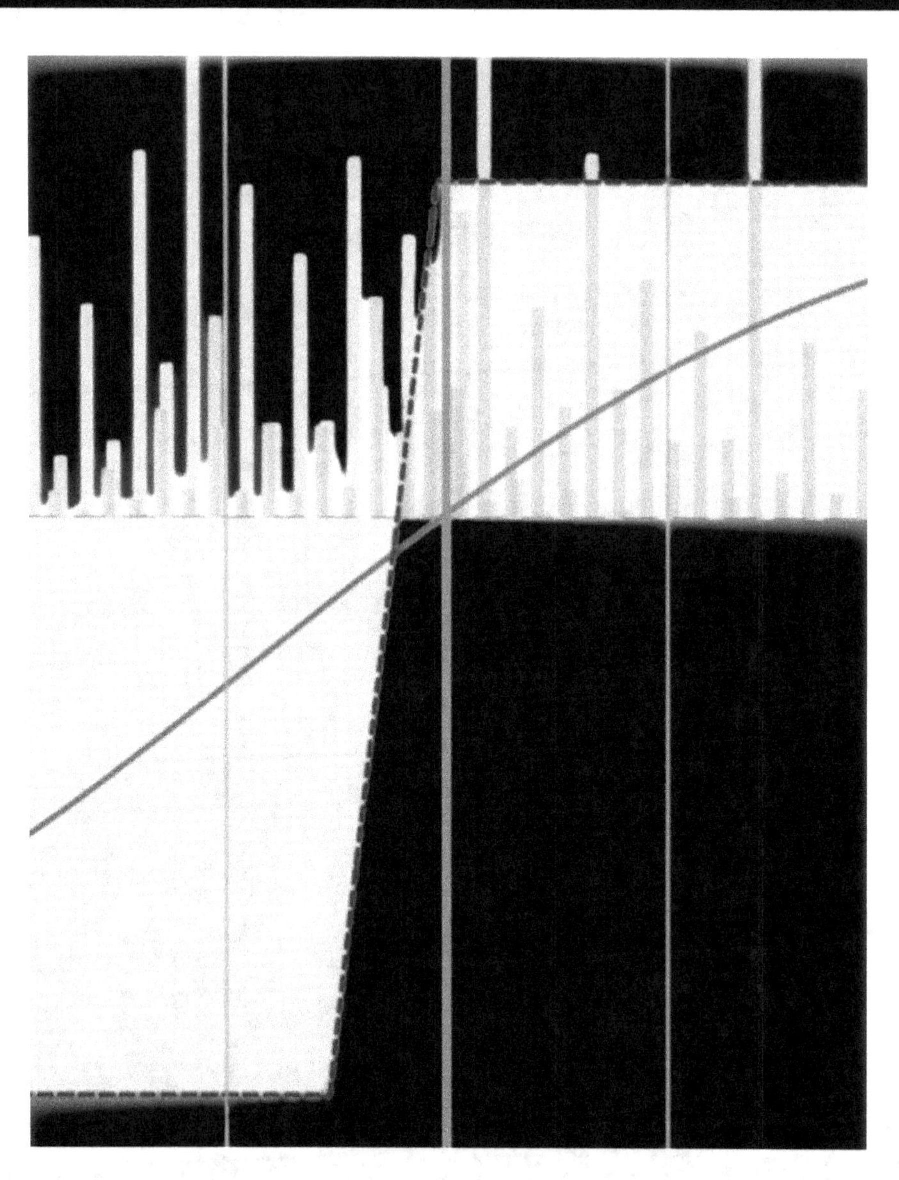

In this graph, you can see that the market protects you for a limited downside while it rewards you as soon as the market gets bullish. Your maximum loss is capped even if your country goes to war and if you are right about the direction of the market, you are bound to earn. Even if you are wrong, but just by a little, to get a flat move, the market will still reward you. Again, time is your only friend in the market. In this case, theta decay keeps you safe even if you are wrong.

Bullish Strategy

Call Ratio Back Spread

Let's assume you are counting on the market to go upwards on the basis of a news, it could be something like the interest cut. Now, the markets will obviously react positively or negatively and you expect a major move on the upside. But, in the market expect the unexpected. What if the news is negative. The entire sentiment of the market will change immediately and a major correction is on its way. While you were expecting, a major upside, you are faced with a major downside. To protect yourself against such instances, the call ratio back spread does wonders. If the market heads in your direction, your profits are unlimited, and if it heads in the opposite direction, you can get a tiny profit or a tiny loss depending on when you are entering. The only thing you need is a move. The only place you make a loss is if the market does not move.

What do you do ?

You sell a call option at the current spot price and buy two call option four slots above the spot price. This protects you on the downside with limited profit while it gives you unlimited gains on the upside.

All you need it to do is move in one direction. If the market does not move at all, you are bound to make a loss. It can move any day until your contract's expiry, but it needs to move. It is better to exit with a tiny profit even on the downside because the market is bound to head for a retracement sooner or later and if it stops at the spot you made your trade in, you are headed for trouble. You can exit in green and reapply the trade at a lower spot price if you still hold a bullish view, giving you the benefit of the retracement as well as the rise.

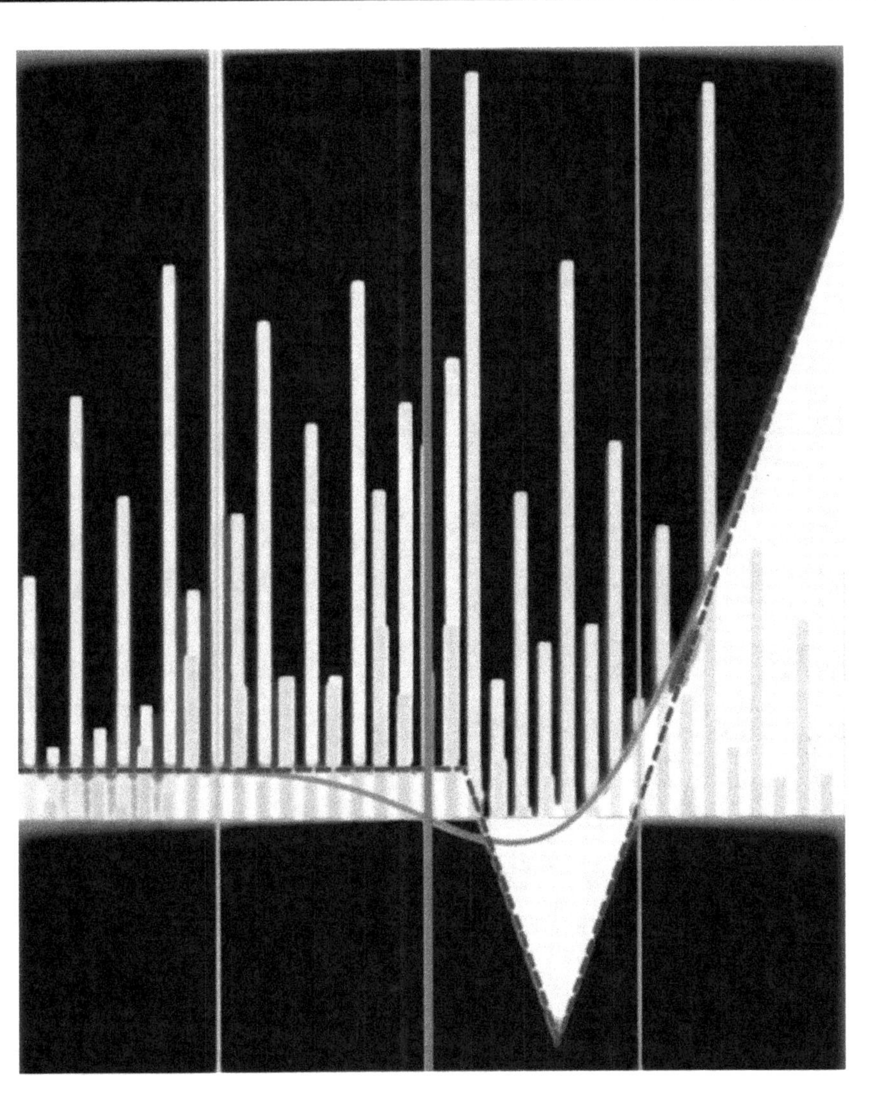

In this graph, you can see that with just a small bullish view, you are in red but if the market goes down, you are still making a profit. In the best case scenario, if the market actually turns bullish, the sky is the limit to your profits. The only disadvantage with the strategy is that in the red zone, the losses are a little more compared to the strategies we discussed till now, but, so is the reward. Your loss is still capped, and that too in small range whereas the on the downside, you have limited profit and if you were right to begin with, the you have an unlimited potential profit. Of course unlimited is not infinite, but is denotes a very high profit that keeps increasing with the increase in spot price.

Bullish Strategy

Long Calendar

Let's assume you have a range bound market, or maybe you expect it to move a little on the upside or even a little on the downside, long calendar is one of the best strategies for such a situation. In this case, the choice is yours, how long do you want to stay in the trade. The more you stay, the more you earn and you are earning on the upside as well as downside as long as you are in a range. The choice of the range will be yours, and you can exit anytime you want. If by any chance, the market moves out of your range in gap up or gap down, where you have no control on something extremely positive or extremely negative, your loss is capped and you are protected on either side.

What do you do ?

If you are bullish, you are biased sideways to bullish, you sell a call option four slots down for the current expiry or whichever you are targeting and buy the same spot price call option one for the month's end. If you are targeting this month's end, buy the call option for the next month's end. In an alternate case, if you are biased sideways to bearish, sell a call option, four slots down for your expiry and buy the month later call option for the same spot price. And, if you are rangebound and want equal protection on both sides, sell the current spot price call option for the expiry you want, and buy a month's later call option for the same price.

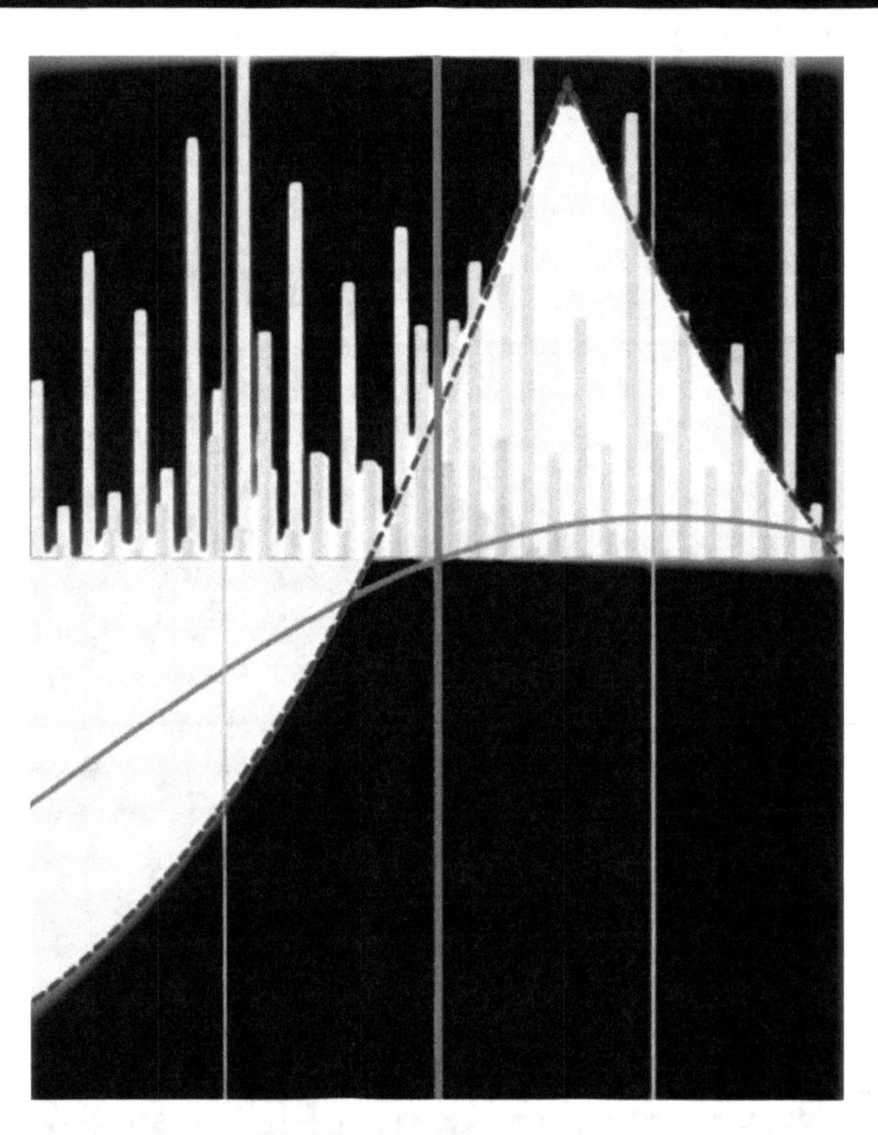

In this graph, you can see that you earn on the upwards side when you buy and sell the slot price four slots upwards while you are still protected on the down side for approximately two slots depending on the expiry. If you sell and buy the current spot price, you will be protected equally on both the sides, and if you are biased sideways to bearish, you will be protected for approximately two slots upwards and earn more on the down side depending on the expiry. If the market moves in your direction, i.e. heads upwards, you earn your target price, if the market falls down a little, you are protected and you earn. If the market breaks your range on the upside or the downside before you can exit, your loss is capped on both the sides.

Bullish Strategy

Bull Condor

Let's assume you are highly bullish, but you are not sure how long it will take. You know you are ready for the market to head upwards, but it can take a few days to get there. This strategy gives you a flat range of maximum profit while highly limiting your losses. You are protected as soon as the market moves upwards in your target range and the profit keeps increasing until it reaches your range of maximum profit. If the market is exiting your range of maximum profit, the profit will start declining until it exits your profitable range, but still the loss on the upper side is capped the same as your initial loss.

What do you do ?

You buy a call option approximately four to five slots above the current slot price and sell a call option four to five slots above your buy. Then you sell a call option approximately six slots above your last sell depending upon the range you are targeting and then buy another call option four to five slots above your recent sell. This hedges your position, minimising your loss and lets you earn as soon as the market enters your range.

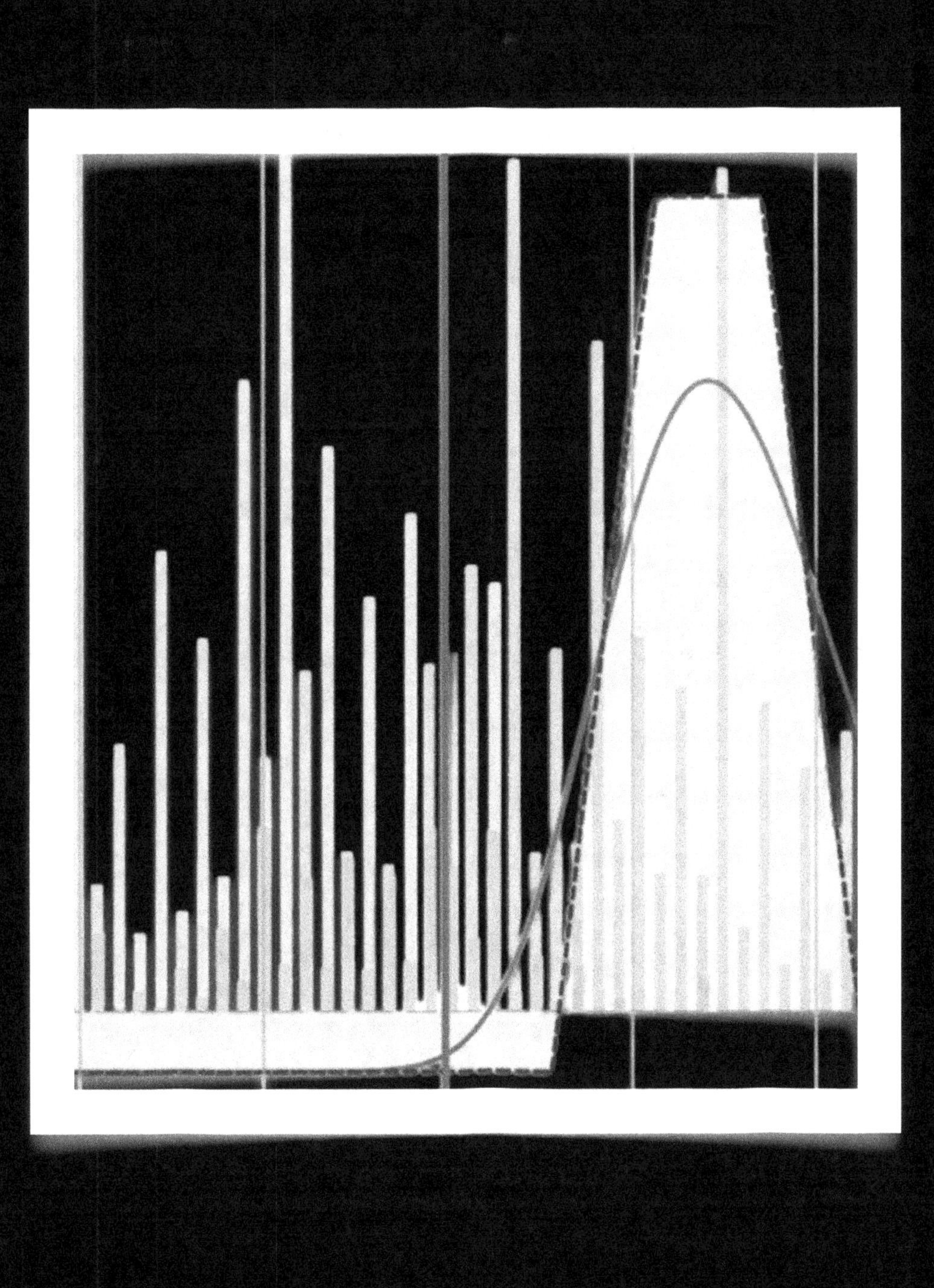

In this graph, you can see that your losses are minimal while your profits start increasing as soon as the market enters the range. They will keep increasing until they reach a flat top of profit range. If you are confident that the market will stay in your range of maximum profit, stay in the trade, otherwise exit with your profit because your profits will start dealing after this until the market breaches your profitable range, bringing you the minimal loss you started with. The advantage with this strategy is that no matter what happens, your losses are minimal and if there is bullish breakthrough a few day later, you have the range to capture the gain. You can increase or decrease the range according to your requirements and expiry.

Bullish Strategy

Bull Butterfly

Let's say now that you are expecting the market to be bullish, but you are not willing to take a huge risk in case you are wrong. You maintain your stand, but you want to be protected in case you are wrong. The bull butterfly does that for you. You get a range where you earn the most at a particular point, but your losses in all the other cases are minimal. You earn the most in the centre of your range, but you are in green as long as the market stays in your target range, but if it does not, your losses are extremely low. The risk reward runs highly in your favour in this strategy.

What do you do ?

You buy a call option approximately four to five slots above the current slot price and se You buy a call option for the start of the range you are targeting. Then you sell two call options approximately two hundred and fifth points above the option you bought, and then you buy another call option another two hundred and fifty points above. This will protect your losses no matter what happens, and give you approximately a five hundred point range to be right. To apply this, just predict a particular spot price where you expect the market to be at your expiry, and then you build your range around it. You will be protected on either side of that spot price with a profit, and even if the market breaches your range, your losses are very limited. ll a call option four to five slots above your buy. Then you sell a call option approximately six slots above your last sell depending upon the range you are targeting and then buy another call option four to five slots above your recent sell. This hedges your position, minimising your loss and lets you earn as soon as the market enters your range.

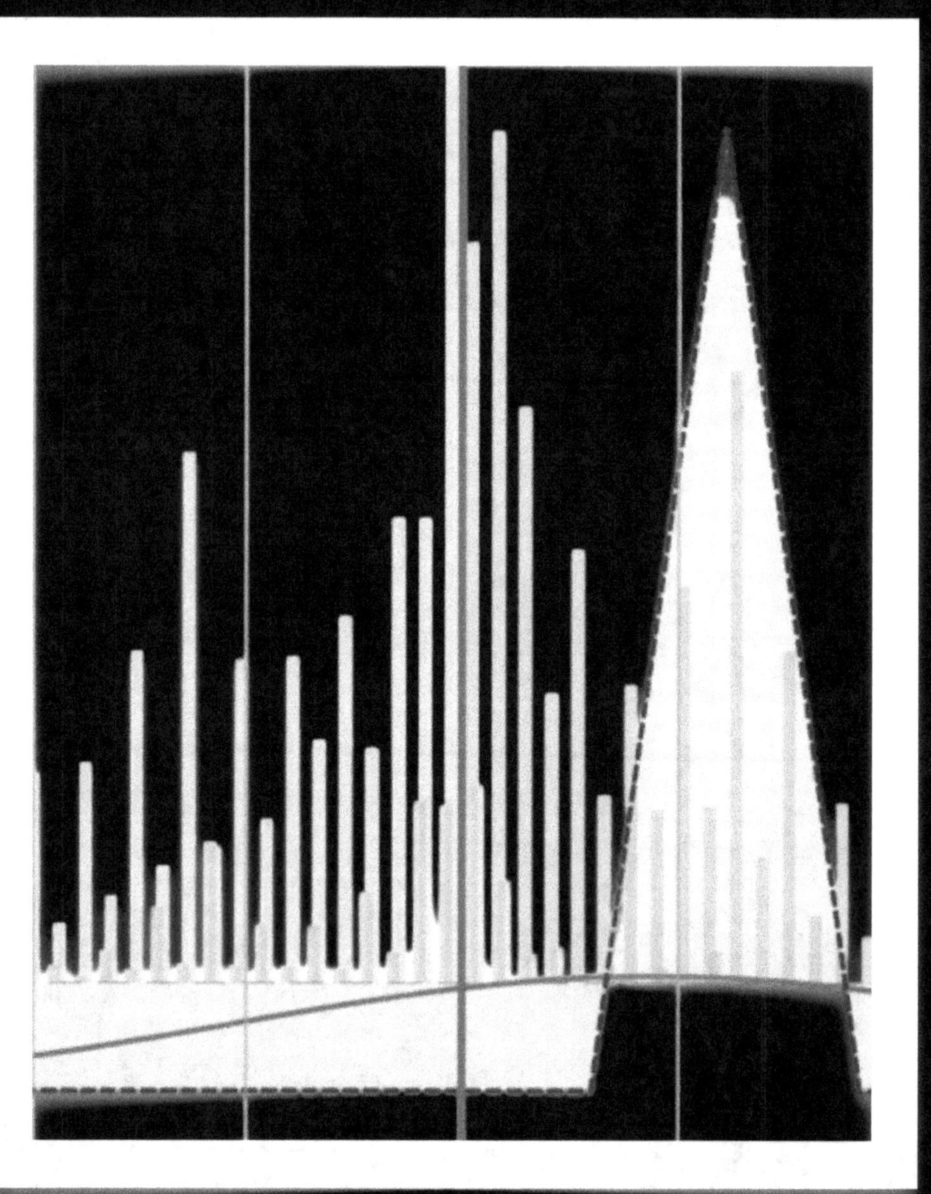

In the graph, you can see that as soon as the market enters your target range, you start earning, and if it expires at your target price, you earn the maximum. Your profit in this strategy can be approximately ten times your potential loss. You can increase or decrease the range as per your requirement or your confidence in your prediction. The increase in range can be directly proportional to your loss cap. This is one of the safest strategies, with a favourable risk reward ratio.

Bullish Strategy

Range Forward

This strategy is not recommended, but if you want to take a risk, it is highly rewardable. This strategy gives you a little protection, but if something goes wrong, it does not have a loss cap. Assuming you are rangebound to highly bullish, this strategy does wonders for you. Here, if you are wrong, you are protected and rewarded for approximately three hundred point on the downside which is a lot and if you are right, you are highly rewarded with a rise in every point. But, if you are extremely wrong, and the market goes highly bearish, nothing protects your downside three hundred points below. With every fall in point, you are going to keep losing as much money as you would have earned on the rise.

What do you do ?

You buy a call option approximately two hundred fifty points above the current spot price, and at the same time you sell a put option approximately two hundred fifty points below the current spot price. This will give you a protective and rewardable range from a few hundred points on the downside to infinity on the upside. Even if the market stays the same, you are bound to earn a little on expiry.

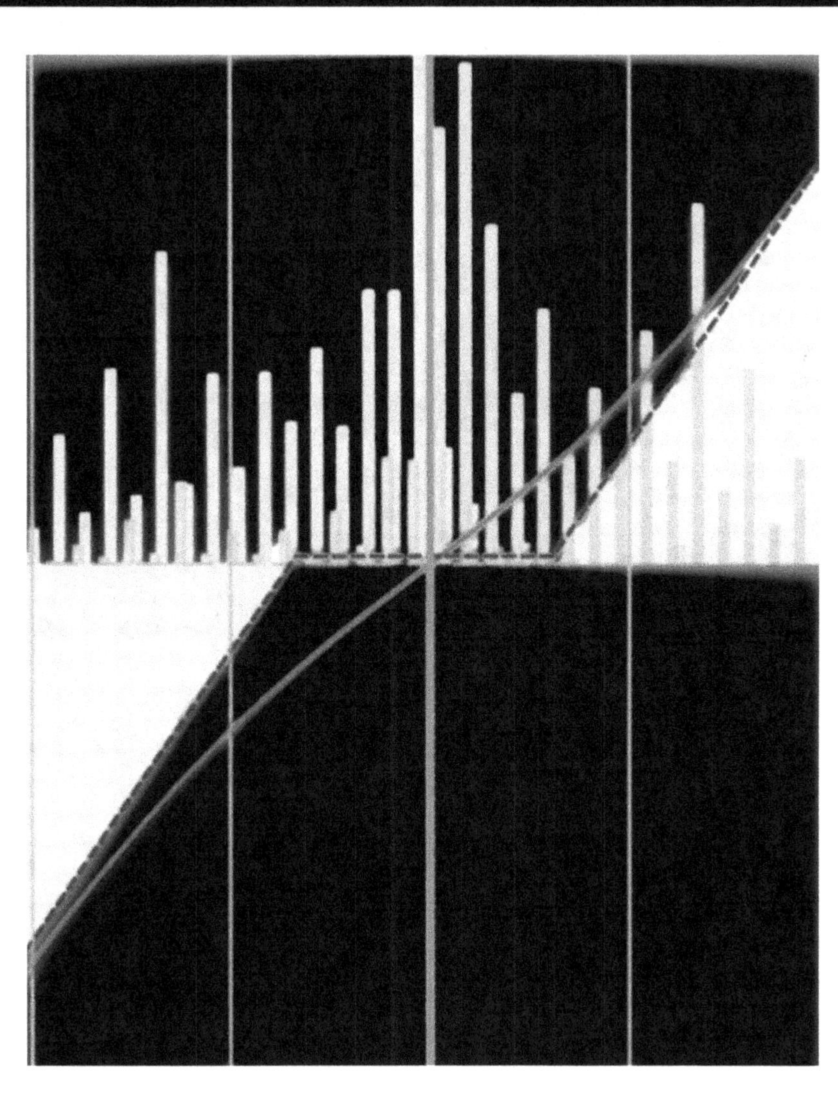

In this graph, you can see that you earn just a little on the downside, but you earn a lot on the upside. This is one of the best strategies if you don't mind the risk, but even though it has an unlimited upside to your profit, it also has an unlimited downside to your losses. Again, this strategy is not recommended, but if you are one hundred percent sure that the market has no major downside till the expiry, and you do not mind taking a risk, this strategy can help you make a nice profit. The major advantage and difference in this from other strategies it that you do not have to wait. Time is almost neutral and you earn per market point. You will not earn more with every passing minute, but you will be constant. If the market moves up, you earn more. If it goes down, you earn less or lose a lot. So, think twice before applying this strategy.

Bullish Strategy

Bullish Hedged Synthetic Future

Everybody who trades in options and has a bad day always thinks I will start trading in futures rather than options. At least the time won't be a factor I will have to consider and the returns are better. But, what if there was a way to replicate your futures with options and that too with a loss cap if you are wrong. In this, your gain will increase just like the options, but if the market takes the opposite direction, you will be hedged against it.

What do you do ?

You buy the call option at the current spot price, and sell the put option at the same spot price. This will become your synthetic future. But, in this strategy, you will buy a put one spot price below. Now, your positions are hedged. If the market follows your bullish direction as you expected it to, you will earn for every point in your favour. In case, the market takes the opposite direction, your loss will be capped no matter what happens.

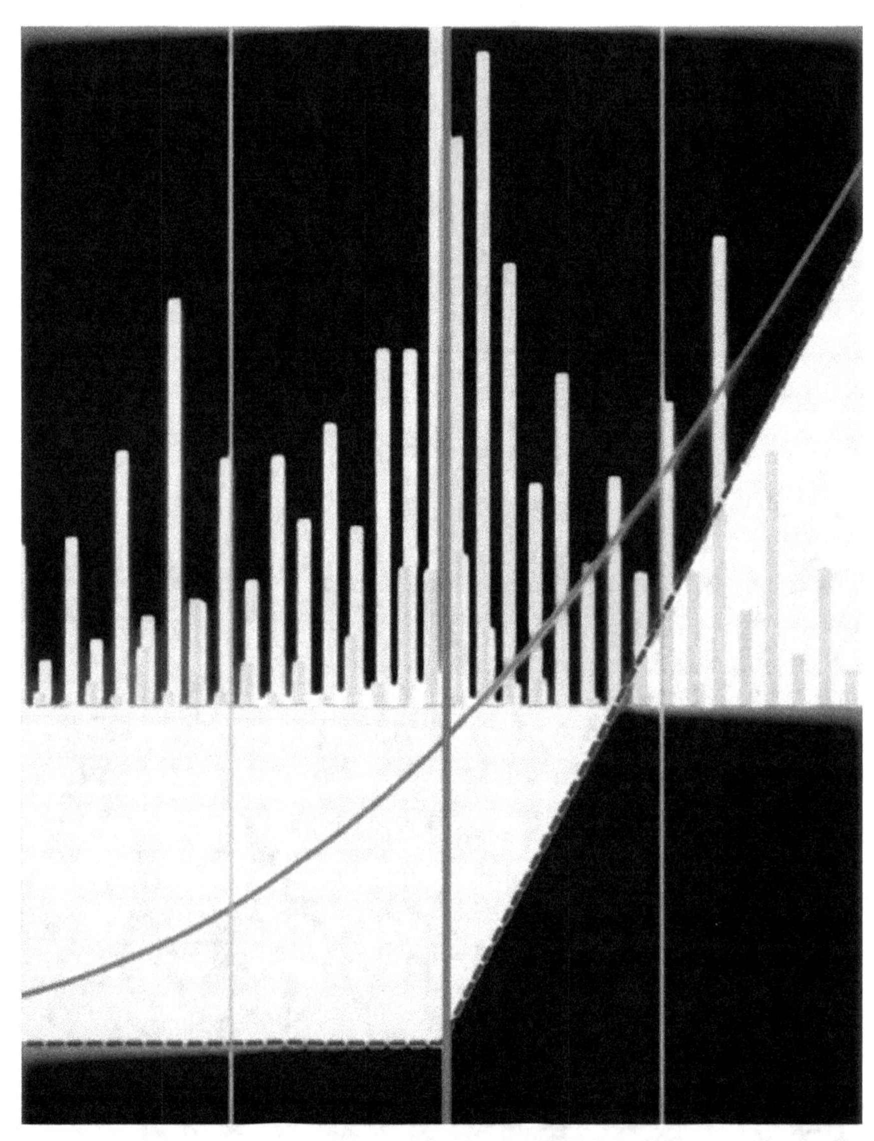

In this graph, you can see that as soon as the market starts heading in your expected direction, you start earning. Here, your gains are unlimited and your losses are capped if the market does not head in your direction. In this strategy, you will have the option to exit with your day's gain or even with your minute's gain, but if you are confident that the market is still bullish, you can even ride it to the expiry. In an alternate case, you can even use this strategies for futures where you buy a future and then buy a put replicating almost the same results. This strategy is really useful when you are working in a 'buy in dip' market.

Bullish Strategy

Hedged Put Selling

Again, selling a put option is the easiest way to make money and is highly discouraged because it is also one of the easiest ways to wipe off your capital. With this, your gain is capped, but your losses are unlimited. To eliminate the uncertainty and protect yourself, you need to buy a put option below the put you are selling. This will hedge your position and your know the maximum gain and maximum loss from your trade.

What do you do ?

You sell a put option at the current spot price, and you buy a put option below the spot price. Now, the choice is yours as to how much you want to risk and how much you want to earn. The lower your hedge is i.e. the lower your buy is below the spot price, the more you stand to gain and the more you stand to lose. The graphical representation for the trade will remain the same and the choice will be yours. Consider how certain you are of the direction and decide accordingly.

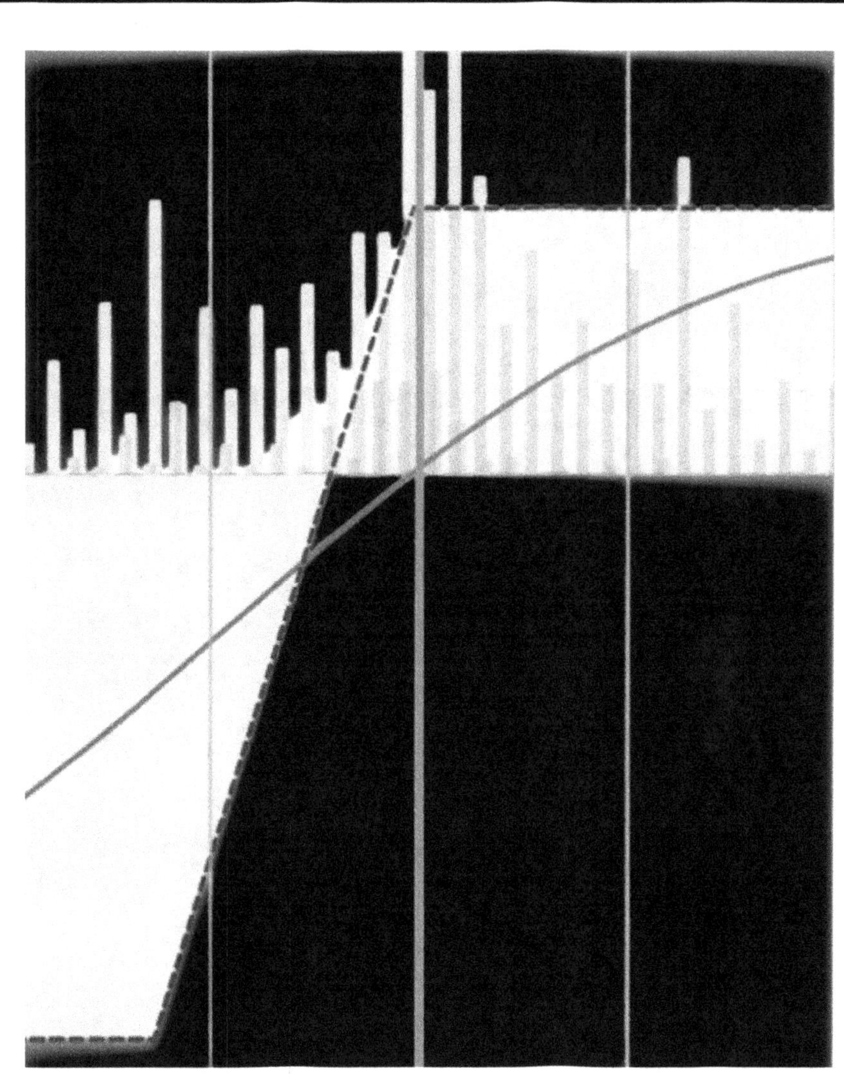

In this graph, you can see that you start gaining as soon as the market heads in your direction, and you will also be protected for a few points on the downside. Even in the worst case scenario, your loss is capped and you just sold a put option and eliminated the unlimited downside. The choice will be yours as to how long do you want to stay in the trade, but the plus side is that time will playing from your team. The linger you stay, the more you gain.

Bullish Strategy

Hedged Call Buying

Everyone who trades in option has once in their life bought a naked option. They might have earned a lot of times, but when they lose, they realise there is no coming back. This is due to the theta decay. Premiums will keep falling and you will have only the market movement to count on. But, what if we can eliminate the theta decay altogether.

What do you do ?

You buy a call option at the current spot price, and you sell a call option at higher spot price. Now again, the choice will be your as to how much you want the risk reward to be. The higher you sell, the more the losses and gains increase. In this strategy, your loss is capped to a fraction of what you would have paid in buying the option and as soon as the market takes your direction, your gain begins.

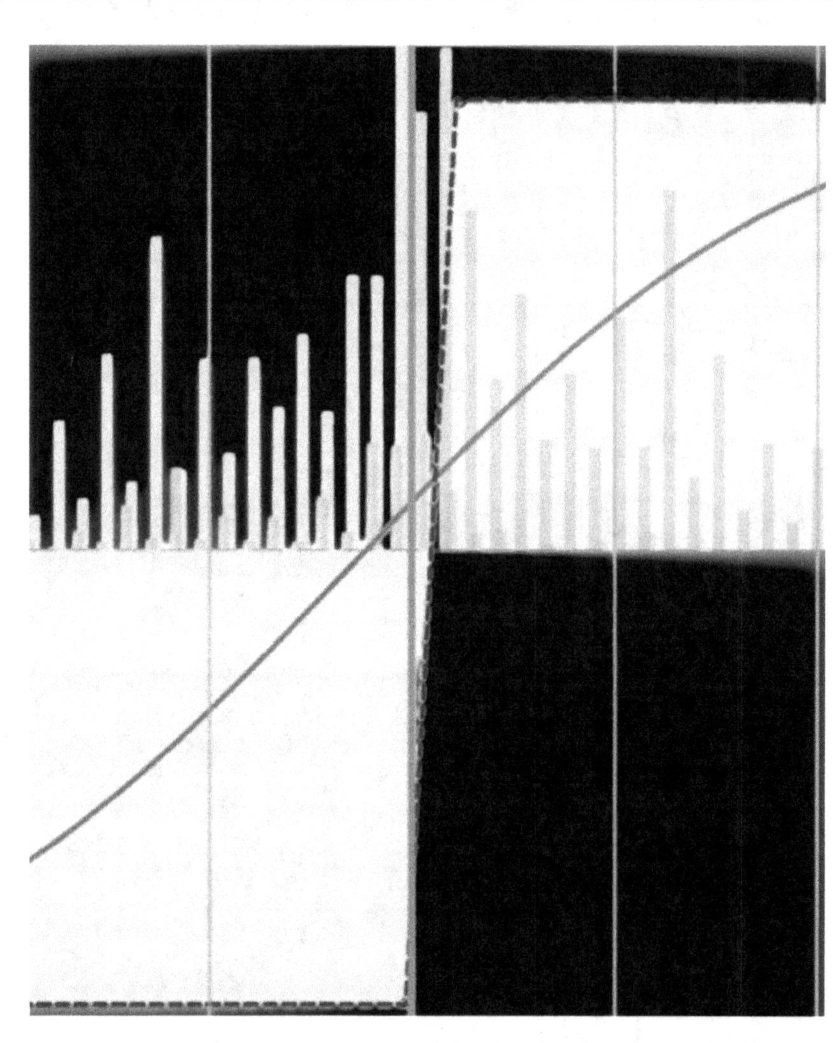

In the graph, you can see that as soon as the market takes your direction, your gain starts coming in and they keep increasing until you reach your range limit. Now, even if you are just a little correct, theta decay will start working for you as long as you are in the trade and your loss will be capped at a fraction of the premium. Your just need to be a little correct for this trade to give you optimum returns, and you can exit any time you want. Again, the longer you stay, the more you earn.

Bearish

Let's say you are bearish from this point, maybe you expect bad results, war somewhere or even a healthy correction. Whatever might be the reason, these strategies will help you earn with your positions hedged. You will know what is the maximum you can lose and how can you earn maximum. These strategies will protect you no matter how wrong you are.

Bearish Strategy

Put Spread

Like the inverse of call spread, if the market heads in your direction, you earn and if it doesn't your, loss is capped. You will start earning as soon as the market goes down, and the longer you stay in the trade, the more you earn. Here too, time will be playing from your side and if you are correct, no matter how long it takes before the expiry of the contract, the market will reward you.

What do you do ?

You buy a put option at the current spot price, and then you sell the put option at the slot about two hundred points below. You can increase and decrease the slot of your buy and that is in proportion going to increase your maximum loss and profit accordingly. The more loss your risk, the better the profit. Think of it this way, when you want to increase your investment, do you want to increase your number of lots or do you want to earn the same with a single lot. Keep in mind, what is it you want to risk and how sure are you of the market'd direction.

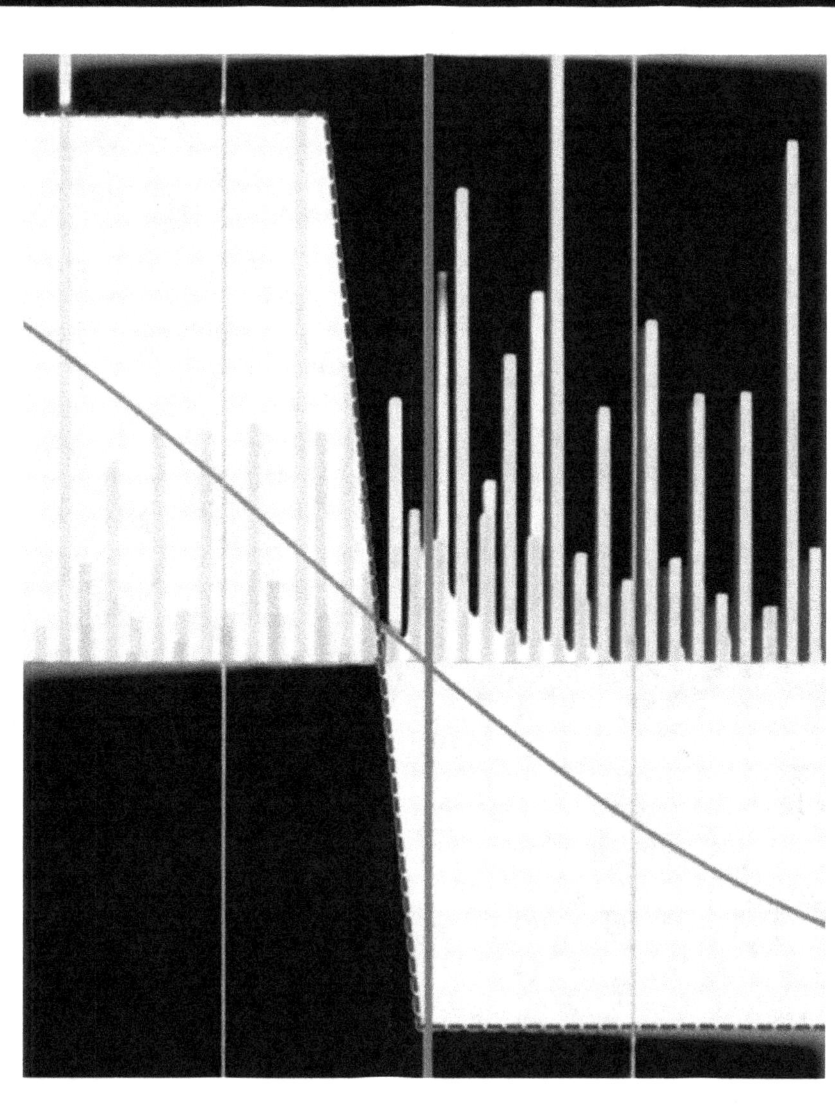

In the graph, you can see as soon as the market takes your direction, you start earning and if you are right for a few points, you will be in green from that point onwards. Now, if you are sure that the market will be rangebound or continue the downtrend after this point, stay in the trade and you will be rewarded. But, if you feel there is a slight possibility of a bounce back, exit with your profit and retake the trade again at a more comfortable spot price.

Bearish Strategy

Call Spread

Call spread replicates similar result to put spread, but with the advantage of letting you be wrong for a few points. If the market does not head in your direction and holds its ground, call spread rewards you anyway. You will start earning as soon as you are right, but if the market does not move, it protects you and even rewards you a little.

What do you do ?

You sell a call option at the current spot price and in turn, buy a call option of the slot about two hundred points above the current spot price. You will earn as soon the market heads in your direction and still earn if it does not, but rather stays in the zone. All the while your maximum loss will be capped and theta decay will work in your favour.

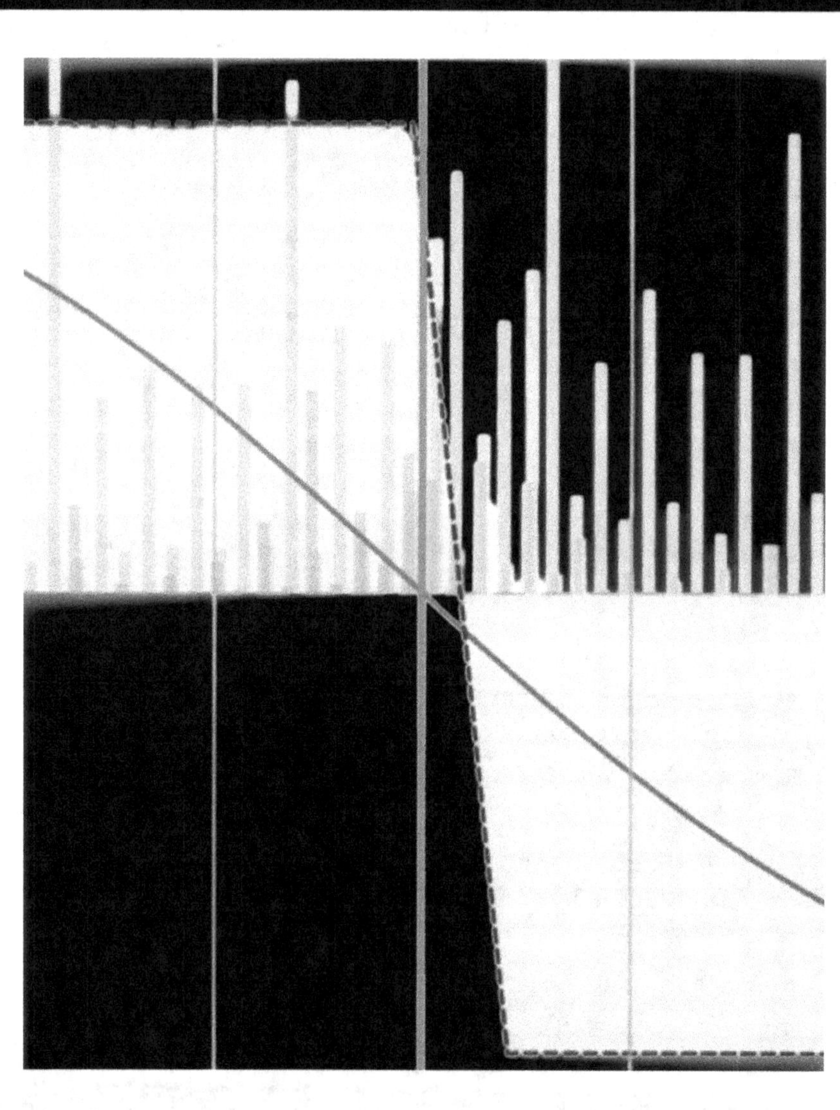

In the graph, you can see that if the market moves a few point in the upwards direction, the strategy still protects you. Although, if the market heads in your direction i.e. downwards, the market starts rewarding you and the longer you stay, the more rewarding is the trade. Your trade will remain hedged, and you can think more confidently about whether you want to stay in the trade or leave with your gains.

Bearish Strategy

Put Ratio Back Spread

If you are sure of a bearish trend, put ratio back spread can fetch you unlimited gains all the while protecting you if you are wrong. The only disadvantage with this strategy is a rangebound market where you will suffer the maximum loss, but that too is capped. With put ratio back spread, just like call ratio back spread, you can have a minimal loss or minimal profit if the market heads in the other direction depending on when you enter, but the market needs to move. If it starts heading in your range as soon as you enter, you start turning green. Here, time is not really your friend, but if the move is right, it can be. If the market stays where it is, you suffer your maximum loss, but if it moves in your direction and breaks the loss range, you can stay as much as you want if you anticipate a further downfall.

What do you do ?

You need to sell the put option at the current spot price and buy two put options approximately two hundred points below. In this strategy, since time is not working for you and if there is even a shred of doubt of market coming to your original spot price, you should exit with a profit. And, you can reenter again at a more comfortable price. In all instances, you need to avoid the market coming back to the same spot price you started your trade in. But, if the market heads heavily in your direction, enjoy the ride because the gains are unlimited.

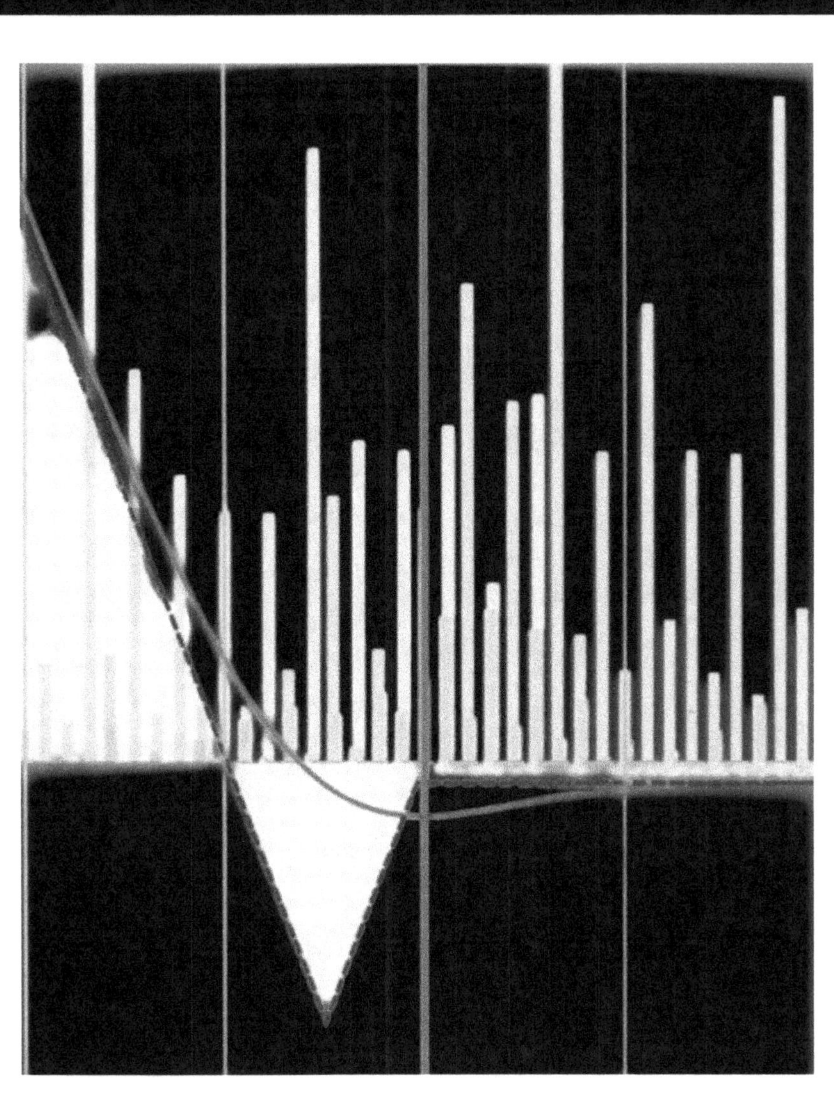

In the graph, you can see that at the current spot price, you are almost protected. If the market heads in your direction, you start turning green. But, you need to break the red range or you need to exit with whatever you have gained. Once you are in the green range and are confident about the market turning rangebound to bearish, you should stay in the trade because you will be highly rewarded. Again, if the market in the green range turns rangebound, you will neither gain anything, nor lose anything. But, if it turns more bearish, you stand to gain a lot. Here, time that initially works against you in the red range, turns redundant as soon as you enter your green range. So, if you are sure of your direction, this strategy can do wonders and most of all, the maximum loss stays capped.

Bearish Strategy

Long Calendar

Let's say you are bearish, but you are no certain of the direction. You are biased towards bearish, but the market is not breaking its support. With the long calendar, you can earn on the downside, and also earn even if you are wrong. This strategy gives you a range, and this range can be as big as you want depending on the expiry, and anywhere the market moves, you gain. Time works in your favour in this strategy, and the longer you stay, the more you earn.

What do you do ?

You need to sell the put option about four slots down from the current spot price for the expiry you are targeting, and also buy the same slot put option a month away from your targeted expiry. Theta decay protects you and rewards you even if you are wrong a little or even if the market is rangebound. If you are right, you start earning instantly and you can exit whenever you want. The longer you wait, the more you earn. The profit will be declining as the market reaches near the end of the range, so you need to exit before the market breaches the range or nears it.

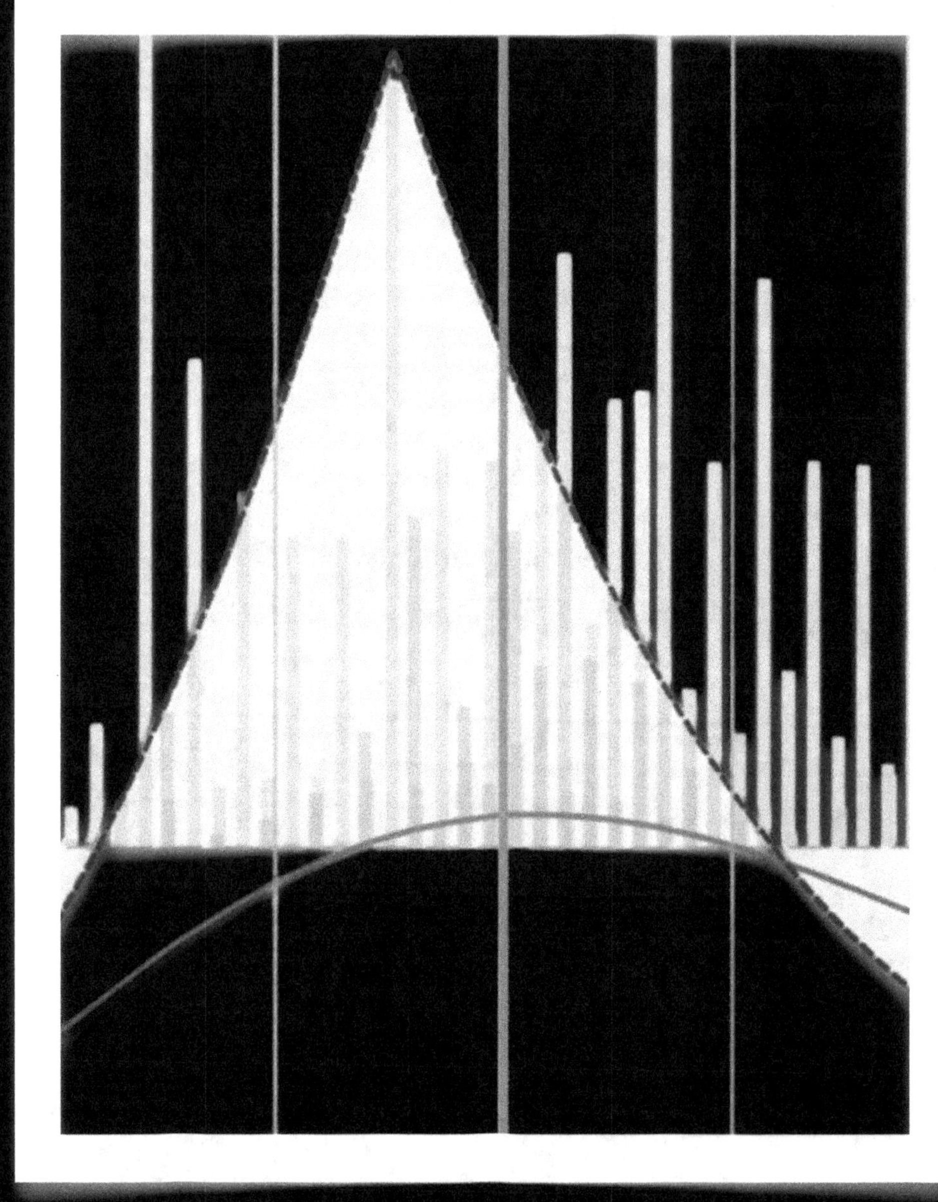

In the graph, you can see that even if the market heads upwards, you are still rewarded, but if you are right you will easily have you range and can ride it out accordingly. Your maximum loss is also capped, but the only problem with they strategy is how far are you from your expiry. Granted, this strategy gives you a big range to stay in, but if you reach the top i.e. where you will be getting your maximum profit, the conundrum will be whether to stay in the trade or exit. Now, you need to predict whether you expect the market to be here or near here in the top half of your profitable range by the expiry, because if the market heads too much in your direction, it will breach your range and you will incur a loss, even though it maybe capped. If you are sure about your direction, you can exit at the top and reenter keeping the spot price in check, because even if you are a little wrong, you will be rewarded.

Bearish Strategy

Bear Condor

Assuming you are bearish on the market, but you want minimal losses if you wrong, this strategy does wonder for you. It gives you a bearish range of profit which keeps increasing as the market moves in your direction, and turns into a top profit before it starts dealing again. Similar to the bull condor, exit when you think your range can be breached or even your top can be breached, and you will be rewarded accordingly.

What do you do ?

You need to buy the put option about four slot under the current spot price, and then sell the put option five slots below your buy. Then you need to sell the put option about fourteen slots or seven hundred points below and then buy a put option about five slots below from this sell. This will give you a profitable range, all the while minimising your loss if you are wrong. As soon as the market enters your range, you start earning and you continue earning till it reaches your profitable top. The top will also give you your own range and if you believe, the market can be rangebound at your top, or even near it, ride the profit because time is in your favour here.

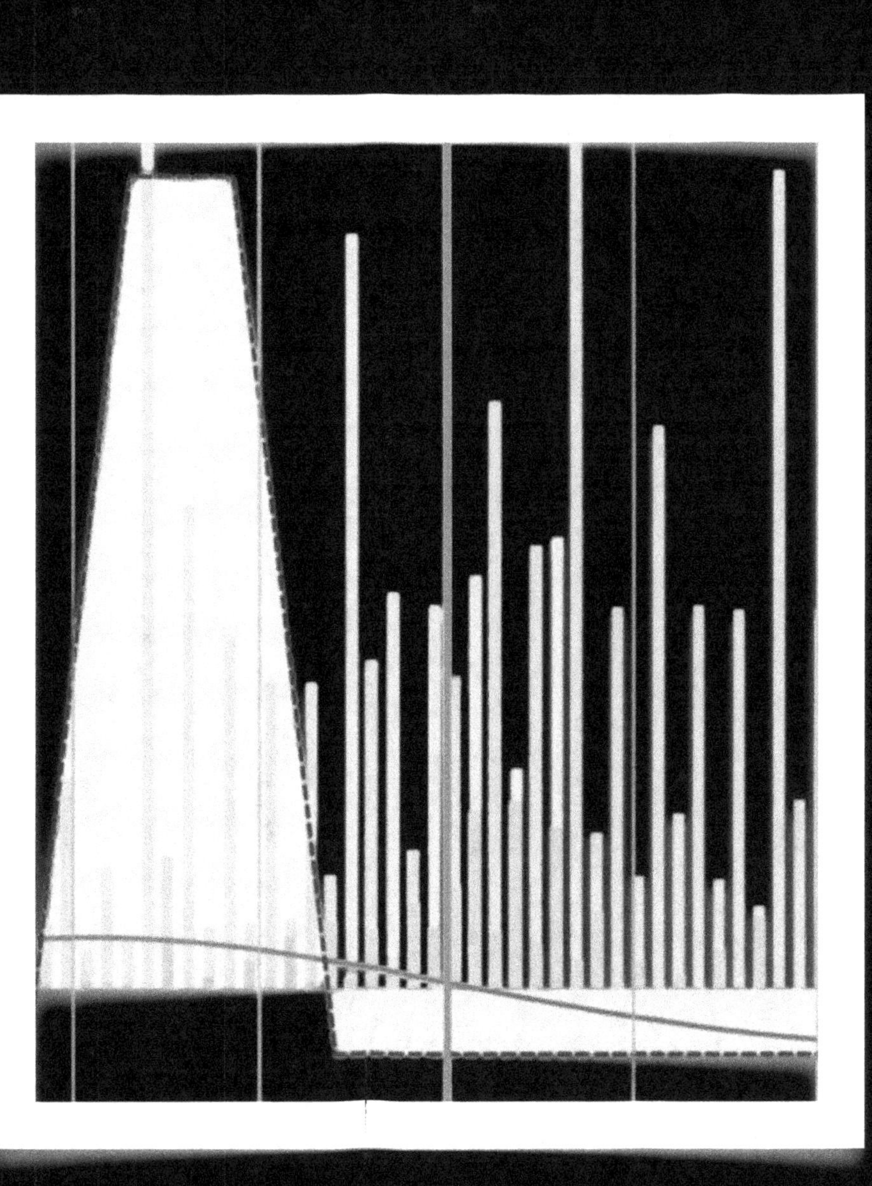

In the graph, you can see that as soon as the market takes your direction, you start earning and if it enters your range, time comes out to help you. The more you stay in the range, the better are your results, and even if you are wrong, your losses are really low. You are hedged on both the upside as well as the downside and you can increase or decrease your range depending on your expiry and your profit target.

Bearish Strategy

Bear Butterfly

Let's say you have a bearish bias, but are not that certain that the market will take that direction. It could be in times of volatility or even news based, but your bias is intact and you want negligible losses just in case you are wrong. The bear butterfly helps you achieve that. You start earning as soon as the market heads in your direction all the while your losses are negligible. You can exit instantly in green or if you gain the confidence that the market is heading towards your target range, you can ride the trade while earning with every point the market heads in your direction until it reaches the top of your profitable range. After that, you need the market to be rangebound to let time do its magic or if you are happy with results and expect some movement in either direction, you can exit with your gain.

What do you do ?

You need to buy a put option about six slots down, and sell two put options another four slots down from your buy. Also, you need to buy another put option about five slots down from your sell. Your position will be hedged and in case you are wrong, your loss will be negligible. You will earn the most in the centre of your targeted range, and the more time passes, the more you earn. Time comes out to play for your team when you are in the target range, but in no way does it play against you.

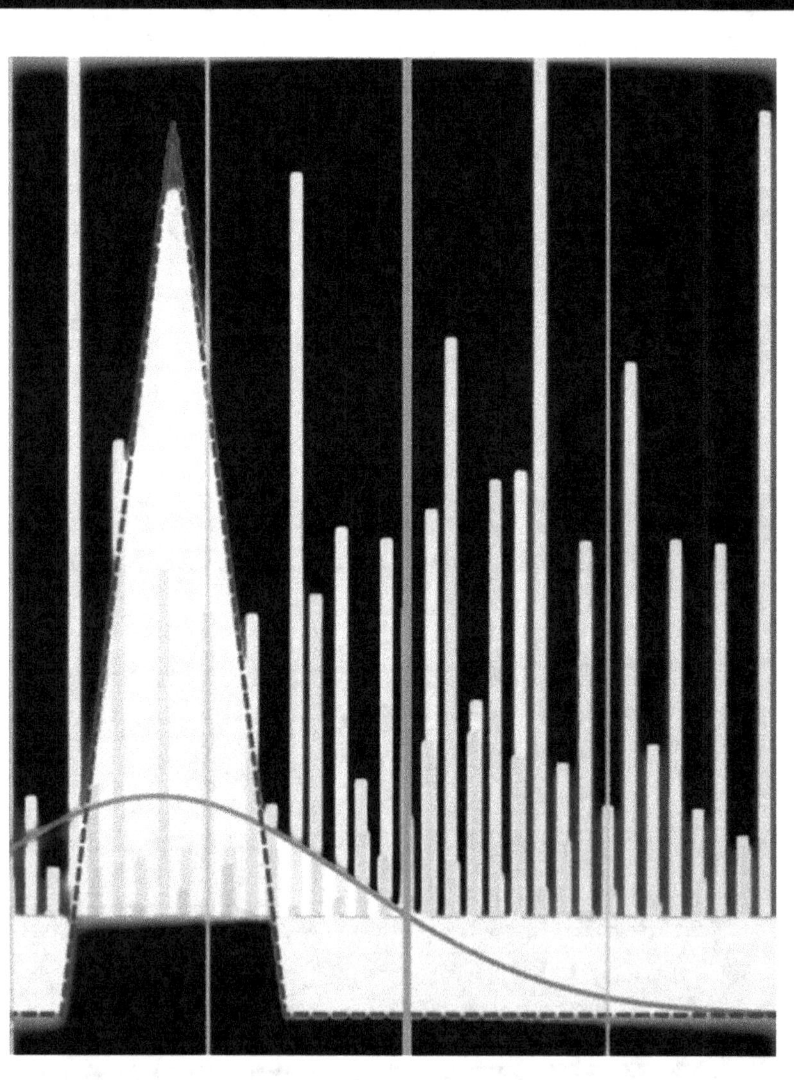

In the graph, you can see that as soon as the market takes a step in your direction, you start earning. But, when the market reaches your direction, the gains start amplifying. This strategy gives you a smaller profitable range, but it rewards you for every point in your direction. If you are not sure that the market will maintain your targeted range, you should exit before you regret it. If you believe that the market will hit your range repeatedly, even if it exits again and again, this strategy will do you wonders as you can exit anytime you are in that range. The later you exit, the higher the reward and in all circumstances, the loss is negligible.

Bearish Strategy

Range Backward

This strategy is not recommended if you have even a shred of doubt of market heading against you. This will give you unlimited and extraordinary gains, but the loss is not capped as your positions are not hedged. This eliminates the theta decay and you earn with every point in your direction. It also protects you for a range in the upwards direction, but if there is major breakout against your position, there might be no coming back from it. This strategy is extremely helpful when you are certain of the market being rangebound to bearish.

What do you do ?

You need to sell a call option about five slots above the current spot price, and also buy the put option five slots below the current spot price. You will be covered and even rewarded for being a little wrong in this strategy, but if you are wrong, it can wipe off your capital. Also, if you are right, it can multiply your capital endlessly. Think of this strategy as buying a put option without the worry of theta decay. You will be rewarded for every point in your direction no matter how long it takes, but in buying a standalone put option, your liability is capped to the price of the premium. In this case, there is no cap on your loss in case you are wrong.

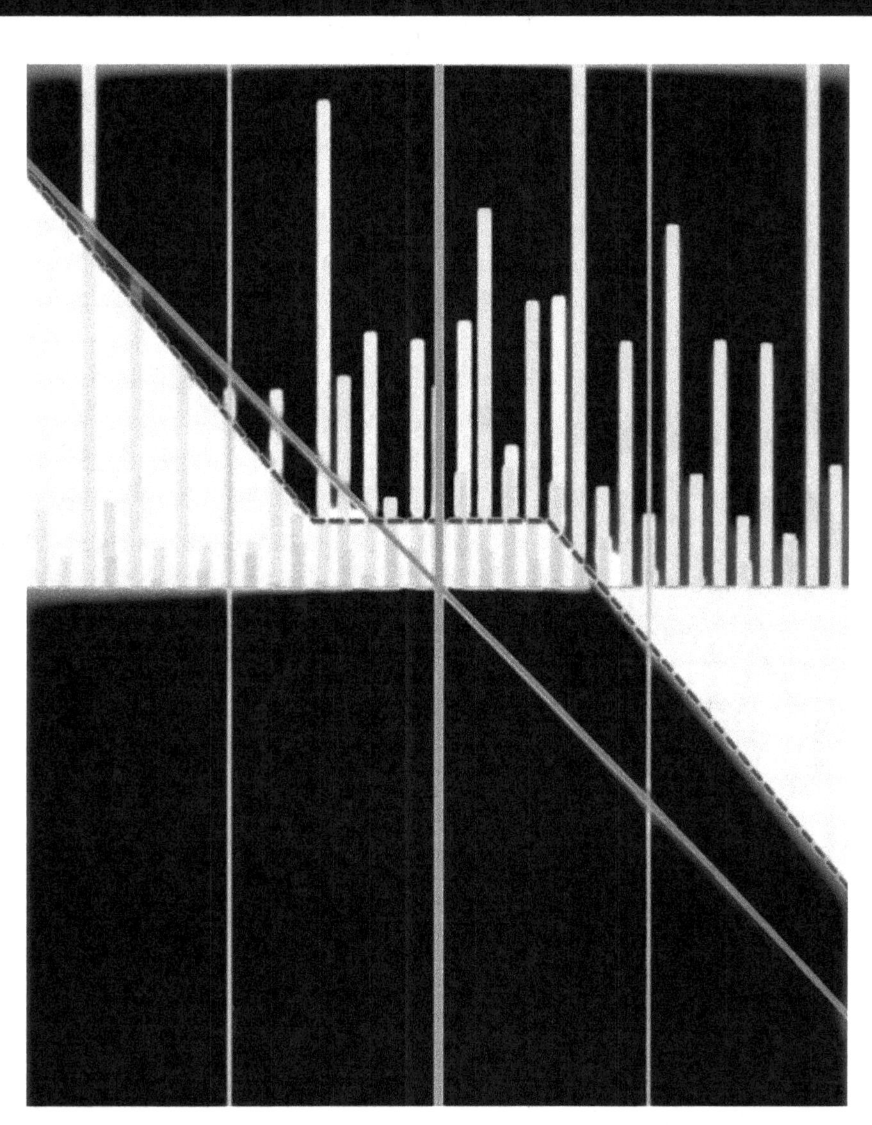

In the graph, you can see that if the market moves against you for a small range, it can be three hundred point to fifty point depending on the expiry you are targeting, you will be covered or even rewarded. But, beyond that breakeven point, there is no end to falling. If the market heads in your direction, that is it takes a downtrend, there is no end to your gains and there is fear of theta decay. If you are deep in the profitable range, and you are still bearish, this strategy is worth the risk of staying in the trade because every point the market falls, you earn along with it and you would have a profitable range ahead to timely exit if things take a turn. But, with every point in the turn, your profits will start decreasing. If you are satisfied with your gain or are skeptical of the direction, you should exit the trade. Again, this strategy is not recommended because of unlimited risk.

Bearish Strategy

Bearish Hedged Synthetic Future

Assuming you are bearish and you want to replicate the results of the futures, this strategy does wonders for you. Because, unlike futures, your loss is minimal and gain unlimited. Your trade will replicate the results of futures and at the same time, hedge your position in case you are wrong. This strategy will do you wonders if your perception of the market is right, but even if you are wrong, your losses will be capped and theta decay will not impact you even if the market takes its time to head there.

What do you do ?

You need to buy a put option at the current spot price and sell the call option of the same spot price. Then, to hedge your position, you need to buy a call option one slot below the call option you sold. This will make you earn with every point in your expected direction and protect you in case the market does not head there. Your loss is capped and your gains are unlimited with this strategy.

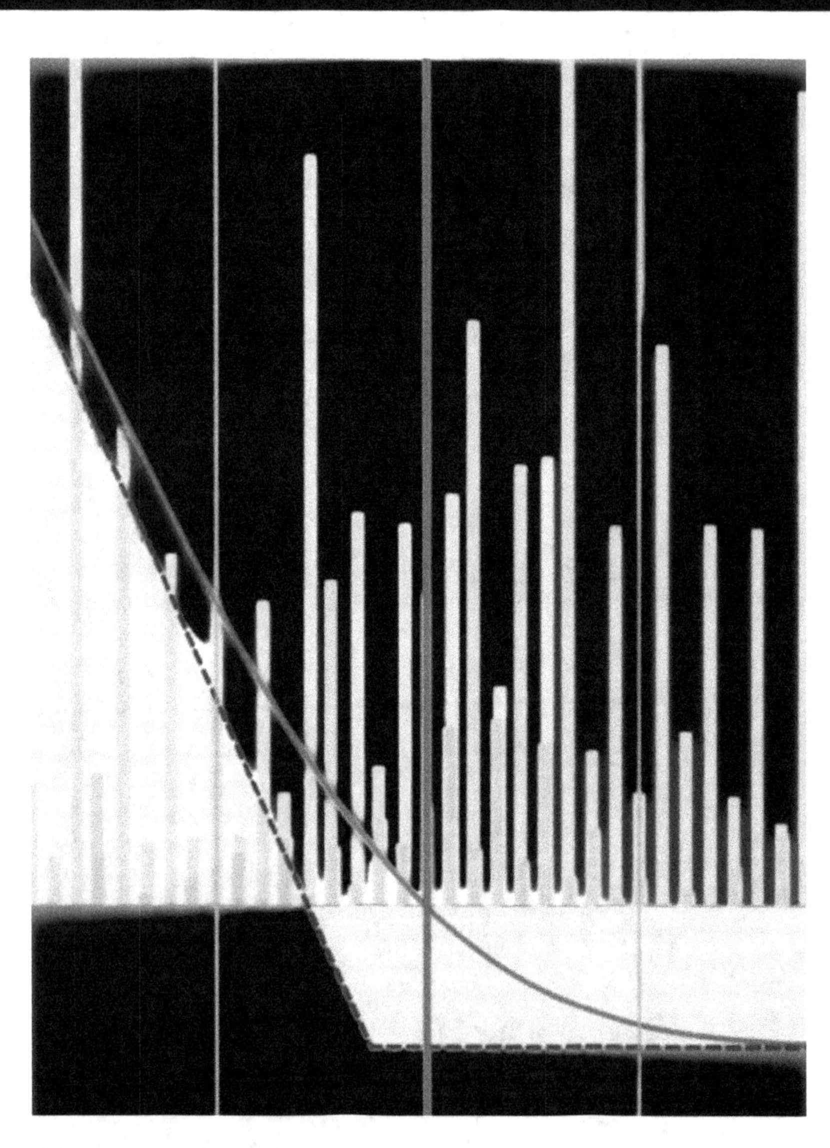

In the graph, you can see that as soon as the market moves in your direction, you will start earning with every point. You will be in the risk of theta decay for a few points, but that will be down the line. If the market makes a move in your direction breaching the breakeven, and you are still bearish, you can ride the trade anticipating a further downside. But, if at any point you see the market changing its direction or breaching your breakeven, you need to exit the trade because you will lose with every point the market moves upside. The gain in this trade is unlimited and the loss capped, so the choice will be yours as to when you want to exit the trade.

Bearish Strategy

Hedged Call Selling

The easiest way to make money in a bearish market is to sell a call, but it also the easiest way to wipe off your capital. If you want to sell a call, it should be hedged and your maximum loss and maximum gain should be known to you before you enter a trade. As long as the market does not breach the call option of the spot price you are selling, you will gain without time being a factor.

What do you do ?

You need to sell a call option at the current spot price or if you are not sure of the direction, sell a call option at whatever price you are comfortable with. Then, you need to buy a call a few slots above the spot price. This will hedge your position and protect you a little even if you are wrong about the market's direction. Your loss will be capped if you are completely wrong and the more you stay in the trade, the better will be the gain.

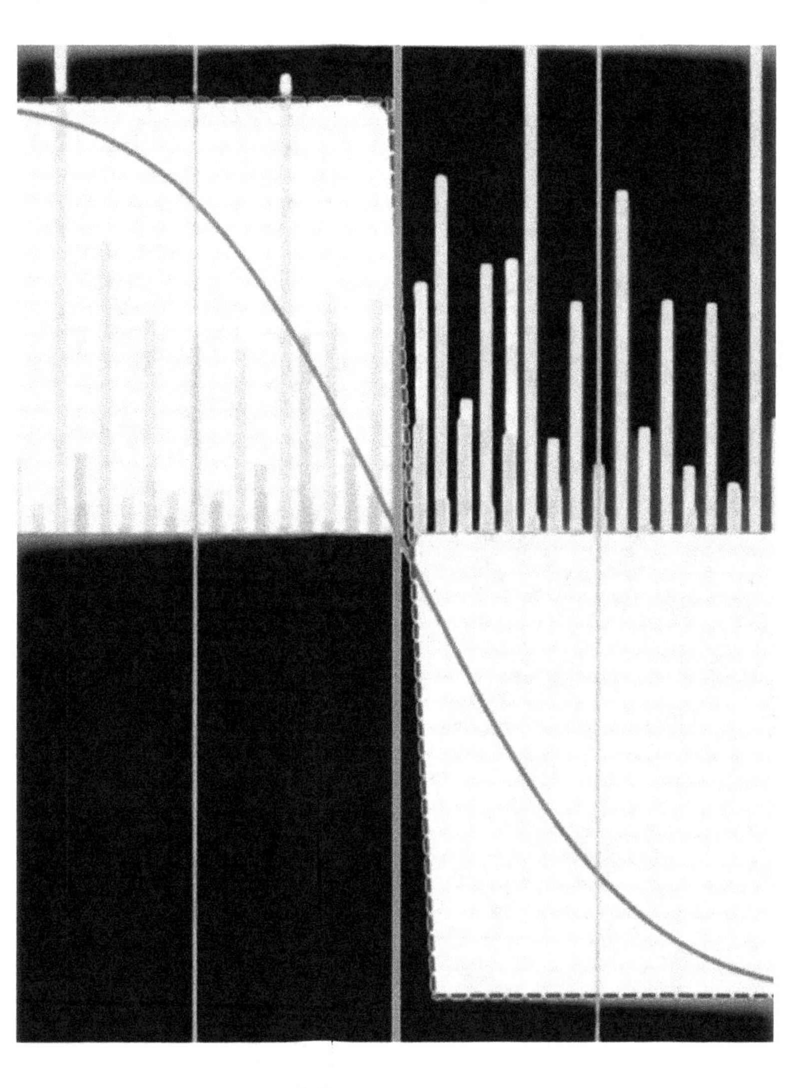

In the graph, you can see that the market starts rewarding you as soon as it heads in your direction and also protects you just for a few point in the upwards direction. In case, you are completely wrong, your loss will be capped and time will let you exit the trade without even reaching your maximum loss. Although, if you are right, time and market will rewards you with every hour, every minute, every second that passes.

Bearish Strategy

Hedged Put Buying

Let's say you are bearish and you want to buy put, but you do not want to fight with time and face theta decay for the time you spend in the trade. Hedging your position will let you do the same. Every option buyer's biggest enemy is the premium decay and this strategy will let you avoid it while capping your loss and your maximum profit.

What do you do ?

You need to buy a put option at current spot price or whatever price you want to trade at, and then sell a put option a few slots down. It could be one two to any number depending on the risk reward ratio you are targeting. The smaller the difference, the lesser is the maximum loss and the maximum profit, but time won't be of any major significance to impact you, but the more time you spend in the trade, the more you will gain.

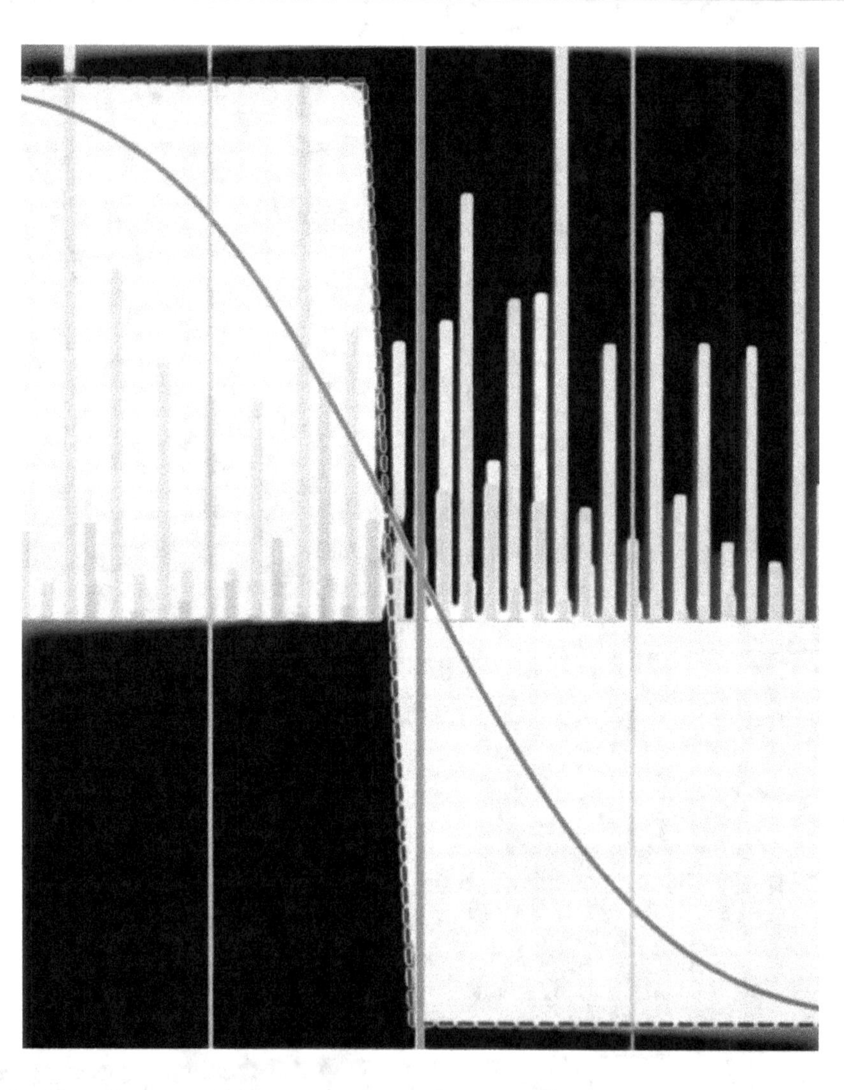

In the graph, you can see that as soon as the market starts moving in your direction, you start gaining until it reaches the maximum ceiling of your profit. Even if the market is a few points down and you are rangebound to bearish, time will get you to your maximum profit. When you are in the green, the further the breakeven point is, the lesser is the risk of staying in the trade and the greater is the reward.

Neutral

Sometimes the market is rangebound or you might be expecting a move in either direction, but you cannot take a decision whether it is bullish or bearish. These strategies will protect you on either side and you will be able to trade taking advantage of time.

Neutral Strategy

Neutral Long Calendar

You can either trade this with call options or put options, depending which side you are just slightly hoping for. In neutral ling calendar, no matter in which direction the market heads, you will be rewarded. Even if the market does not move even a single point, you will still be rewarded and at that point, your reward would be maximum. Also, your loss will be capped if things go wrong.

What do you do ?

Trading with call options, you need to sell a call option for the expiry you are targeting at the current spot price. Then, you need to buy a call option a month away or for the month's end at the same spot price. This will give you the benefit of theta decay along with the protection of market movement in either direction while hedging your positions.

In this graph, you can see that you are protected on both the sides when you sell and buy the current spot price. If you are bullish and you buy and sell four slots above, you will be protected approximately for two slots below depending upon the expiry, and vice versa if you buy and sell four slots below. But, if you are rangebound with this strategy, no matter which way the market heads with a limited move, you earn something. Again, the longer you stay, the more you earn. And, in the worst case scenario, your loss is capped.

Neutral Strategy

Short Iron Butterfly

Assuming you are sure about the market being rangebound, and you want to capture that theta decay while not taking a risk, this strategy helps you achieve your goal. Your risk will be negligible and your reward can be extraordinary depending on how precise you are.

What do you do ?

You need to sell both the call and put options at the current spot price. This forms your straddle that captures your theta decay, but you need your positions to be hedged, so you buy a call option four slots above and sell a put option four slots below. You can shift your buy's upwards or downwards depending on how much you want to risk, but the difference should be equal from your sells. This will give you your maximum profit in the centre of your range while capping your losses to negligible.

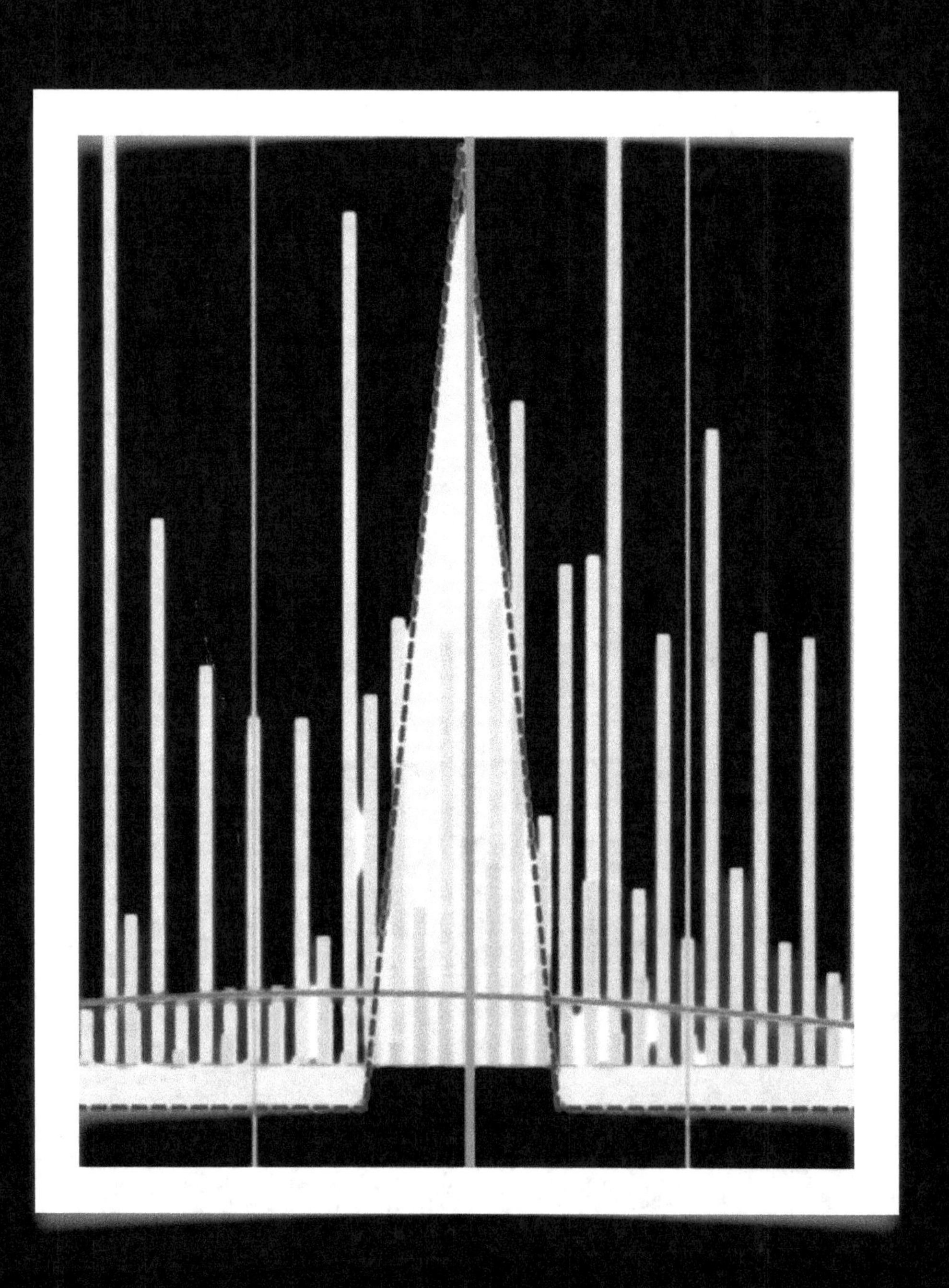

In the graph, you can see that your losses are negligible and at the current spot price, your gains are extraordinary. The gain will decrease on either side, but as long as you are in the range, you will be gaining every second, every minute and every hour. The more precise you are, the better will be the reward and the more you stay in the trade, the more you will be rewarded.

Neutral Strategy

Short Iron Butterfly

If you are certain about the market being rangebound and want to minimise your losses without the hassle of being precise like in the iron butterfly, the iron condor is the perfect strategy for you. It gives you a better range and a flat range of maximum profit, all the while capping your loss to a minimum.

What do you do ?

You need to sell the call option four slots down from the current spot price, and then buy the call option another four slots down. Similarly, you also need to sell the put option four slots above the current spot price and then buy the put option another four spots above. This will give you a big profitable range and also, a flat range of maximum profit along with hedging your positions.

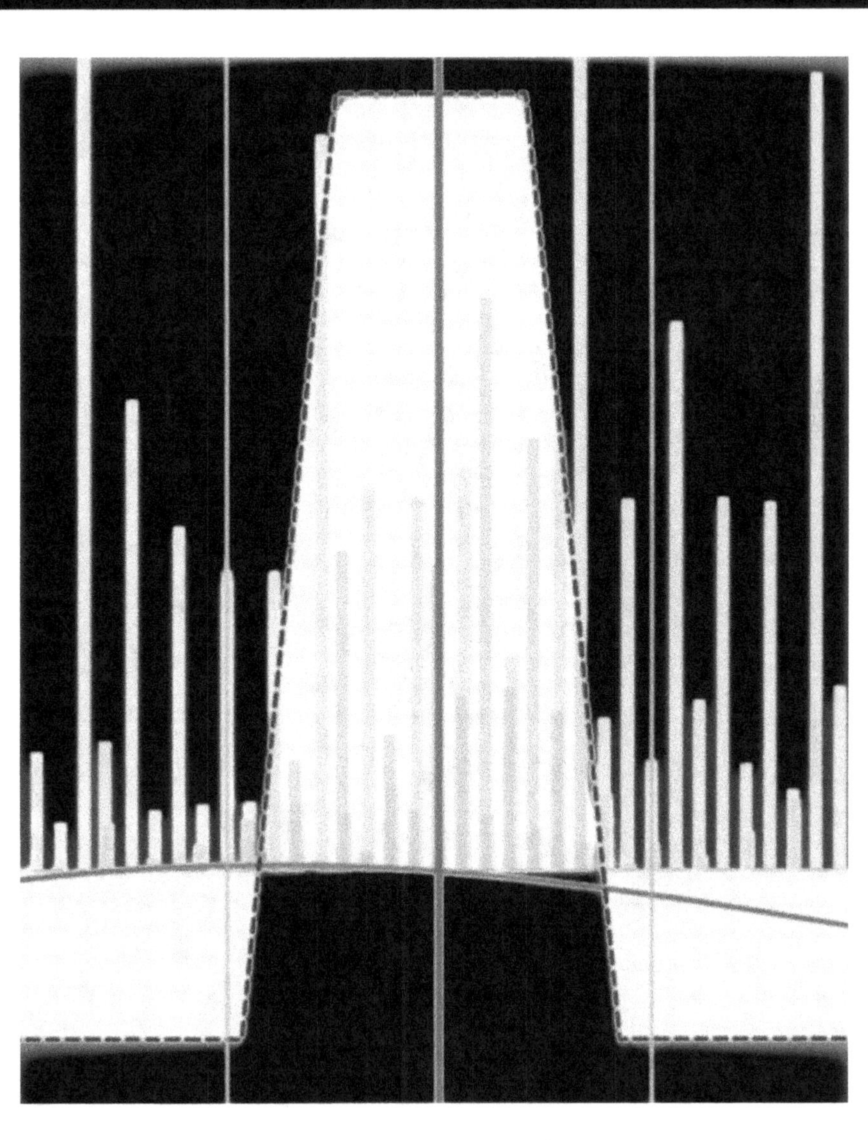

In the graph, you can see that as long as the market stays in your range, time will keep rewarding you for every second that passes. Also, you have your own mini range inside your profitable range where you earn your maximum profit. Even if the market somehow breaches the range, your loss will be capped at a minimal value.

Neutral Strategy

Hedged Batman

This strategy is fairly complicated but it does do wonders in a rangebound strategy. In every other strategy, the closer you are to the edge of your range, the lesser is the profit, but in this strategy, the closer you are to the outside, the better the gain. This strategy gives you the benefit of theta decay on either side while protecting your losses.

What do you do ?

You need to buy a call option about five slots above the current spot price, and then sell two call options one slot above your buy. Then you need to buy a call option four slots above your sell. Now that you are done with call options, you need to buy a put option about five slots below the current spot price, and then sell two put options about one slot below your buy. Then, you need to buy a put option about four slots below your sell. This will form a pattern of Batman's ears and mask along with the benefit of capping your losses.

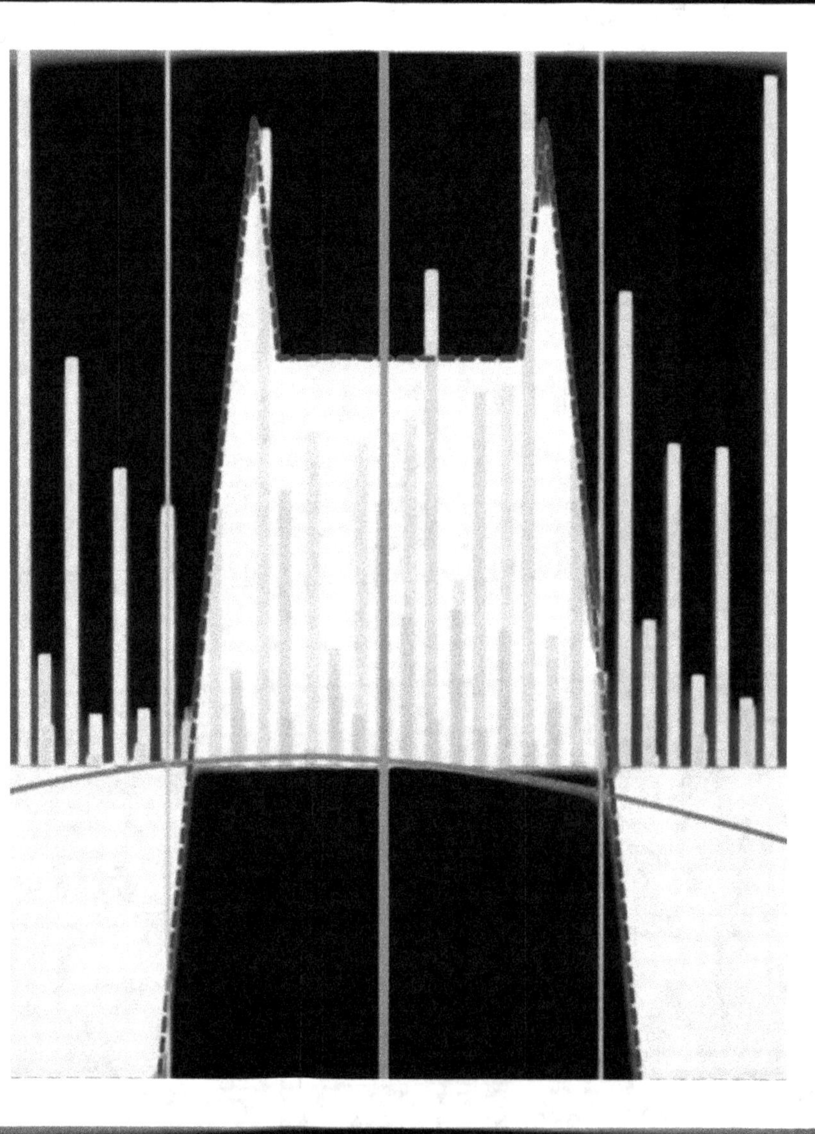

In the graph, you can see that as long as the market is in the range, you will be rewarded for every second that passes. But, if the market gets to the edge on either side, that is the ears area, that will be where you will get your maximum profit and allow you a clean exit, just before the market heads out of your range.

Neutral Strategy

Double Plateau

If you expect the market to not be rangebound, but make a move in either direction, it might be bullish, it might be bearish, but it moves anyway and without facing any decay, this strategy promises you a fine reward. Think of it as two condors in one strategy. It will be complicated, but it will reward you on movement towards either side.

What do you do ?

You need to buy a call option about five slots above the current spot price, and then sell a call option about five slots above your buy, and then sell another call option another five slots above, and then buy another call option another five slots above. Similarly, you need to buy a put option about five slots below the current spot price, and then sell a put option another five spots below your buy. Them. You need to sell another put option another five spots down, and finally buy another put option, again five spots down.

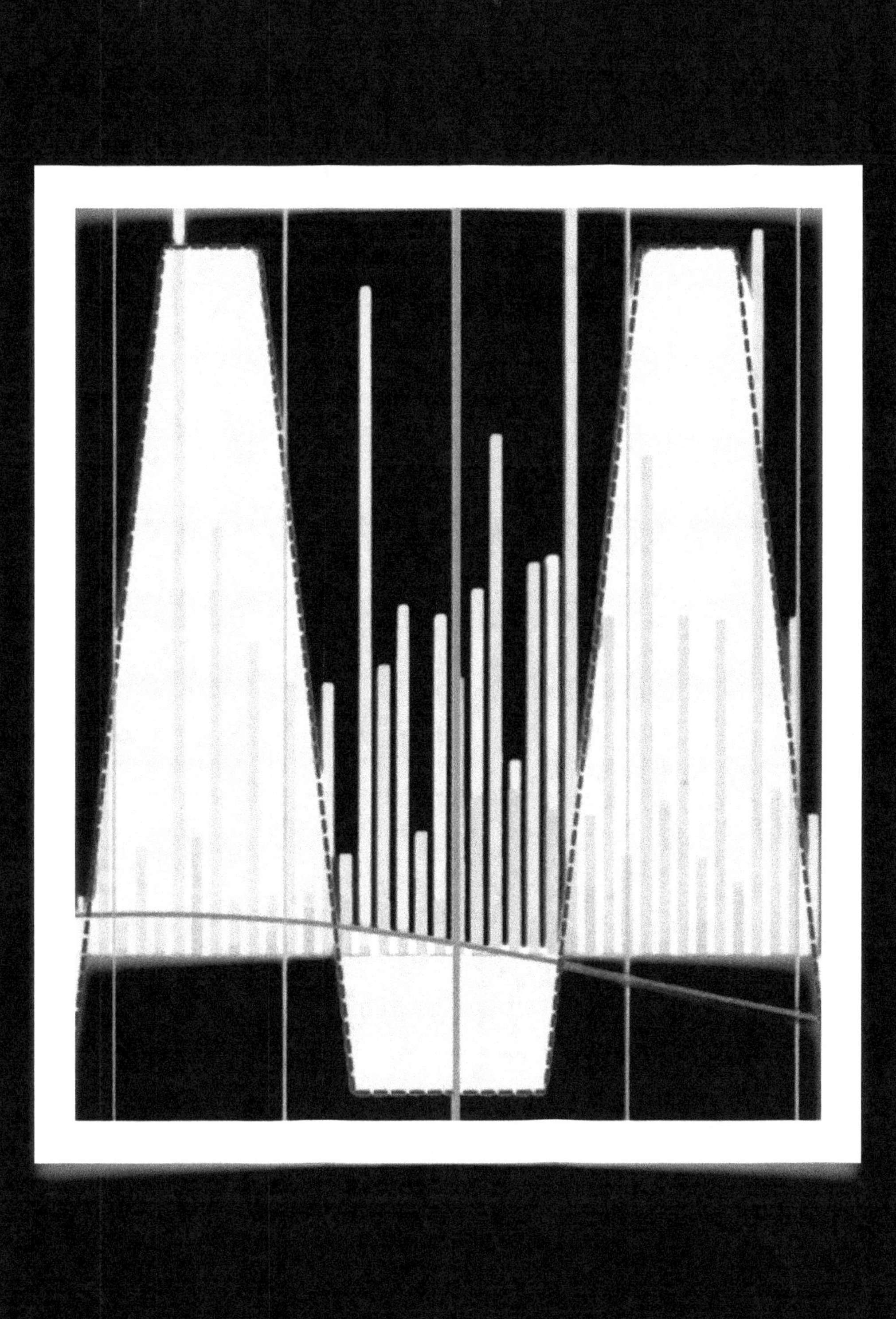

In the graph, you can see that no matter which direction the market takes and no matter how long it takes to get there, you will be rewarded on either side. The profitable ranges will have their own mini range where you will have the maximum profit, and if in any case, the market does not get to your range or even breaches past your range, your maximum loss will be capped and equal in all circumstances.

Neutral Strategy

Hero Zero Long Straddle

Sometimes you are certain of the market making a big move in a certain direction. This works best on the day of expiry, and most of the times when you see the market, you can predict whether a move is likely or not. This strategy will only work if there is a movement. If the market remains flat after your point of entry, you will lose the premium on both the sides, but, the direction of the move is irrelevant for you to gain.

What do you do ?

You need to buy the call option and the put option of the current spot price as cheap as you can. On the day of the expiry, the premiums are melting rapidly, and that is where you need to make your entry. The total of both the sides of the premium must be less than two spots to give you the optimum results. The market can be highly down or highly up, either way if you feel there is a retracement coming soon, this is the best strategy to address that, and again your loss is capped.

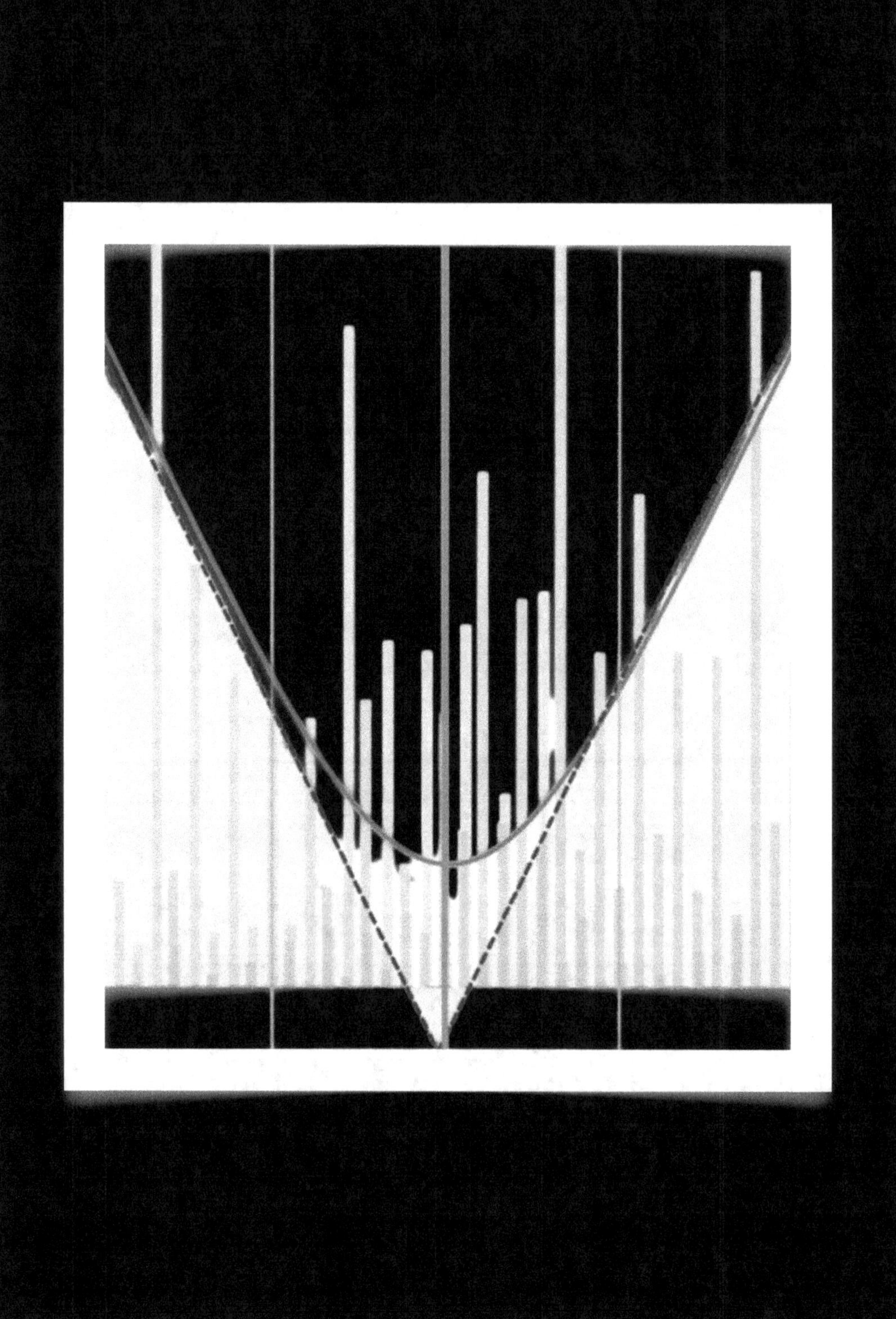

In the graph, you can see that whichever way the market heads, you start earning, and as soon as the market moves beating what you paid for the losing option, your gain becomes permanent and unlimited. This strategy is a high risk strategy as you have the time constraint of expiry, but that is overcome by the cheap option premium.

Long Iron Butterfly

If you are sure about the market breaking range in either direction, the long iron butterfly is a good strategy. Here, you need to predict where the market will not be, and you earn. As correct as you are, the lesser the loss, and if you can avoid the range completely, you get a fixed gain. Here the loss is possible loss is more in comparison to the profit, but the market movement works in your favour.

What do you do ?

You need to buy the call option and the put option at the current spot price, and then see the call option about four slot above and the put option four slots below. This will hedge your positions while giving you a flat gain on the market breaking the range.You will lost the maximum at the spot price you are entering the trade, anywhere else the market is at any point of time, you will be better off or most likely in green.

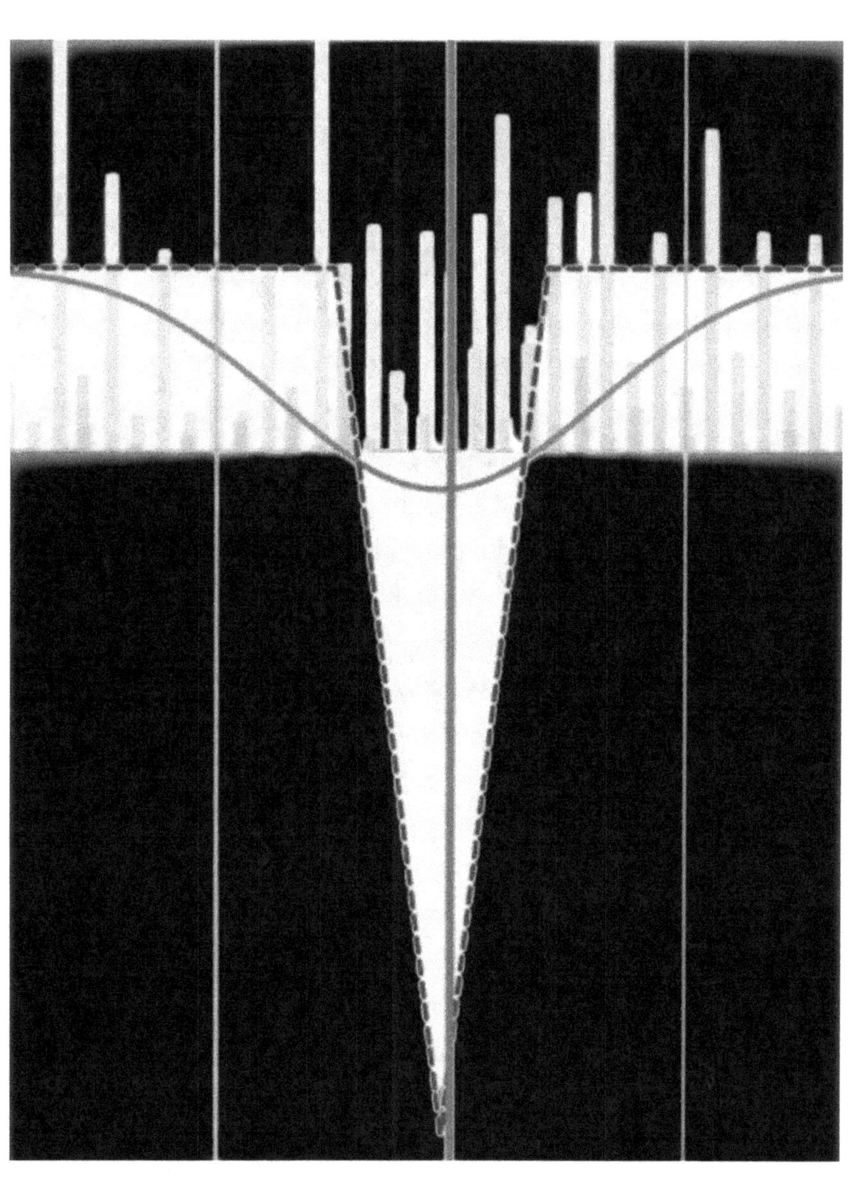

In the graph, you can see that as soon the market exits your red range, you will start earning, and once you are in the green range, the market and the time start working for you to reward you. The only place you can lose is if the market does not move.

Neutral Strategy

Long Iron Condor

If your view still remains a breakout in either direction, and you don't want to predict a point of maximum loss, but want some consistency of gains as well as losses depending on the breakout, long iron condor helps you with that. Here, your loss is capped as well as your gain. While the iron butterfly makes you play with a smaller negative range, in the iron condor you need to dabble with a bigger range.

What do you do ?

You need to buy a call option about four slots above from the current spot price, and then sell a call option another four slots above your buy. Similarly, you need to buy a put option about four slots below the current spot price, and sell a put option about four slots below your buy. This will give you a negative range to play with, but anywhere else the market goes, you stay in green.

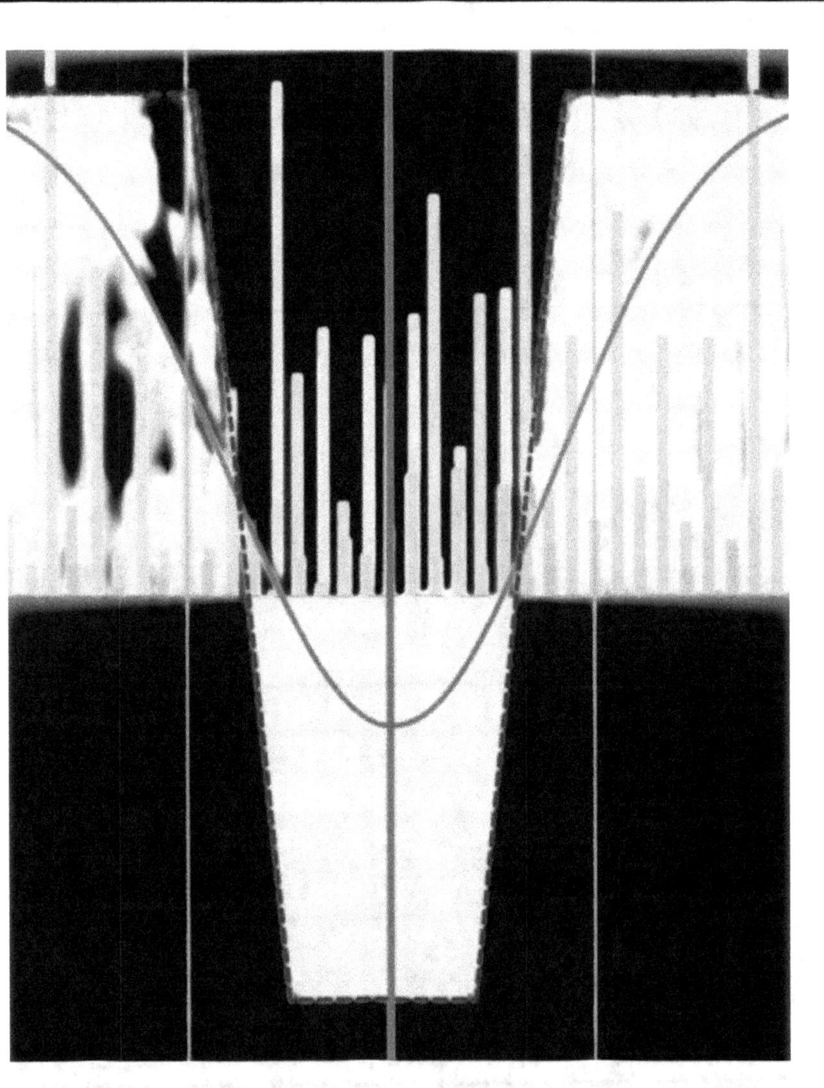

In the graph, you can see that as soon as the market breaks your red range, you start gaining and time and market let you gain more with every second that passes by and every point in your favour. Once, you enter the green range, you need to evaluate the chances of the market returning to the red range, because as time passes by and it rewards you accordingly, if you go back in red, you will be penalised accordingly. The maximum gain and maximum loss is similar in this strategy depending on when you enter, how far is the expiry and how far is your hedge.

Neutral Strategy

Long Strangle

If you are certain if the market moving, and do not want to risk a lot in buying the current spot price, the long strangle helps you earn from the market movement, provided the market breaks a range you set before entering the trade. The gains are unlimited, and the loss is capped but time is slightly biased against you in this trade.

What do you do ?

You need to buy a call option about four slots above the current spot price and also buy a put option about four slot below the current spot price. This gives you a flat bottom loss in your range, but as soon as you break the range, the gains have unlimited potential. This strategy cannot be worked on the day of the expiry because a movement this big is unlikely on the same day, and cannot be predicted.

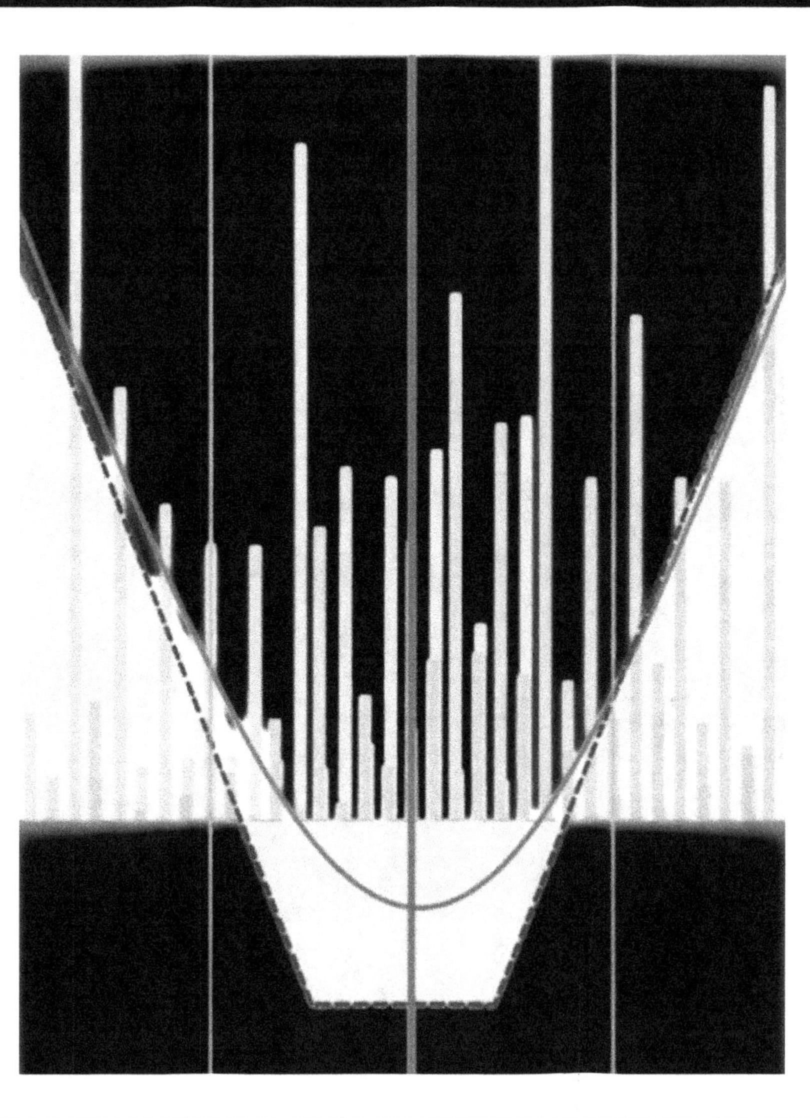

In the graph, you can see that as soon as the market breaks out in your green range, the gains keep rising on the either side and time becomes irrelevant, but if you are in the red range, time will work against you and you will lose money with every second that passes. Compared to the long straddle, if you are comparing to enter at the same time, the risk is lower in they strategy while gains are unlimited in both the strategies.

Neutral Strategy

Strip

Let's say that you find the market at a point where a big move is coming, and that is based on upcoming news. You expect that news to be negative, and accordingly a downfall. But, there is still a chance of that news turning out to be positive, and the market rallying accordingly, strip will help you earn in both the sides, but if the market does not move in either direction, it will also bring you heavy losses.

What do you do ?

You need to buy a call option at the current spot price, and buy two put options at the same spot price. Now, since you started with a bearish move, you will start earning on the downside sooner that the upside, but you will earn with big movement in both the sides.

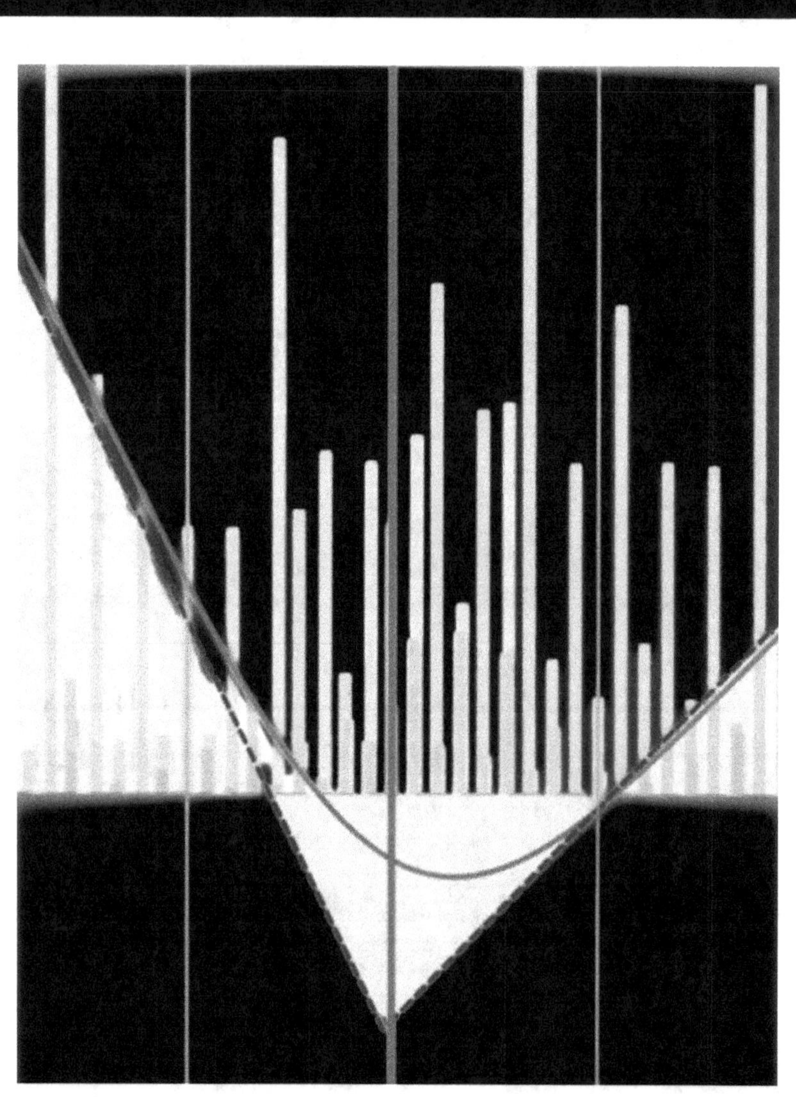

In the graph, you can see that if the market heads down, you start earning, and if the market heads upside, you will still earn, but you will need the market to travel a longer distance for it. The gains are unlimited on both the sides and the loss is limited, but the loss is heavier than most hedged strategies because time will work against you here in the red range.

Neutral Strategy

Strap

Keeping the factors of strip in mind, but taking a bullish view, strap lets you earn on both the sides, but you will earn more and sooner in the uptrend. Again, your loss is capped here and your gains are unlimited. Strip and strap work best with news anticipation, whether it is rate cut or election result. A trigger does wonders for this strategy.

What do you do ?

You need to buy a put option at the current spot price, and also buy two call options at the same spot price. As soon as the market makes a move in your direction, you start earning heavily. But, if the market takes the opposite direction, you will still earn. This is the worst strategy in a sideways market, but possibly the best strategy in a volatile market.

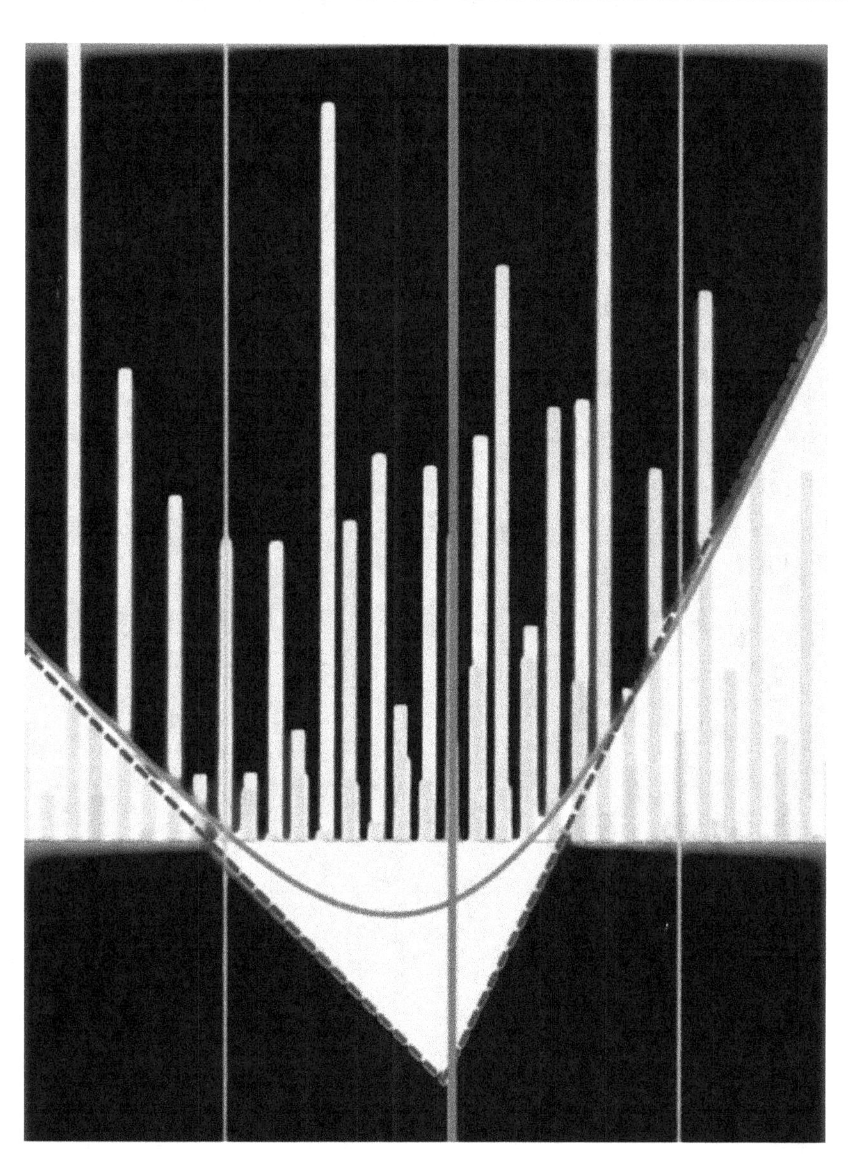

In the graph, you can see that your gains are unlimited on either sides, but the only problem comes with the market being rangebound because losses are heavy in this at the current spot price and expiry. Also, time becomes redundant as soon as you enter your green range, but you need to be aware of retracement to the current spot price, because as soon as you enter the red range again, time will work against you.

Neutral Strategy

Mix & Match

The mix and match strategy will be completely your prerogative and there is no fixed set of rules to implement it. The goal here is to earn maximum while limiting your loss to as lower as you can. This strategy can be implemented to any strategy that you want to play with, but your exit will be sooner than you anticipated while the gains will be more.

What do you do ?

You need to mix the calendar months in your strategy. Let's say you want to use the bullish hedged synthetic future, but you are not comfortable with the maximum possible loss the strategy provides. The bullish hedged synthetic future is buying a call option at the current spot price, selling a put option at the same spot price and then buying a put option one slot below. Now, here if you are targeting the month end expiry, you can replace your put buying with the coming week's expiry or wherever you are comfortable, and if you are right, you will earn more and if you are wrong, you will earn less. The

What do you do ?

The only thing that gets reduced here is the time. If you had time till the month's end to be right about it, you will get till your bought put option's expiry. But, upon reaching near your hedge's expiry, you still feel you are right and the market will head there, you can take out the profit of your hedge for this expiry, and buy another put option at bought call option and sold put option's expiry. This continues your hedge at a possible lower price, and the gives your profit from your mid month hedge, while also giving you time to prove your prediction right.

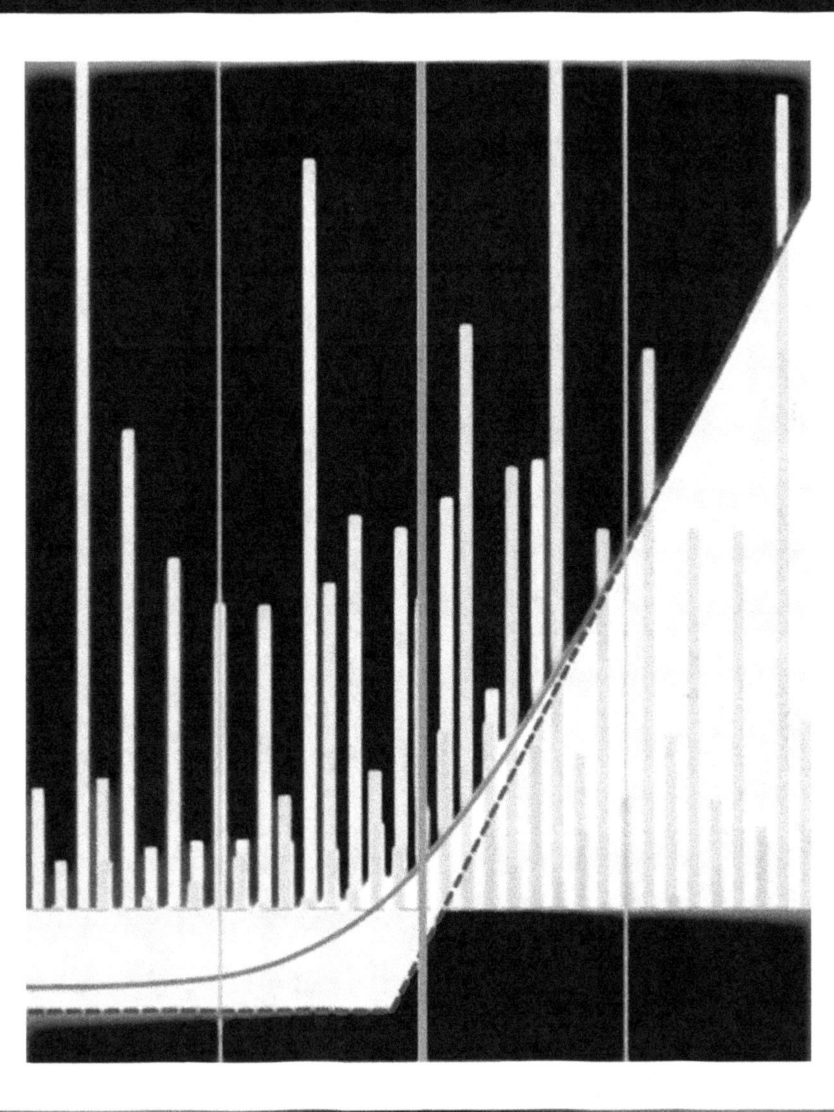

In the graph, you can see that as soon as you right, the market rewards you and if you are wrong, the hedge protects you with lower losses. If you are right, the loss is irrelevant in both the cases, but if you are wrong, the mix and match saves your losses drastically. This strategy can be applied to any of the other strategies, but the decision will have to be yours depending upon the expiry, your predicted market direction and the time you want to get there.

All strategies have been made taking 25,000 points as basis and 50 points as a slot. If you are trading in a substantially different point index, adjust the slots or points according to the spot price.

Strategy

Write your strategy here

Your personal strategy
Your personal Mantra

Write it down
You will need it soon

Futures and Options Cheat Code

THE FUTURES AND OPTIONS TRADING CHEAT CODE

Mantras that will always protect you no matter what happens

Time to steal from the **Operators** in their own game

JK BULL

Stock Market Cheat Code

THE STOCK MARKET TRADING CHEAT CODE

Mantras that will never let you lose even a single dime

Time to cheat the **Operators** at their own game

JK BULL